'Race' and the Primary School

Theory into Practice

'Race' and the Primary School

Theory into Practice

Bruce Carrington and
Geoffrey Short

NFER-NELSON

Published by the NFER-NELSON Publishing Company Ltd.,
Darville House, 2 Oxford Road East,
Windsor, Berkshire SL4 1DF, England.

First published 1989
© 1989, Bruce Carrington and Geoffrey Short

British Library Cataloguing in Publication Data
Carrington, Bruce
    "Race" and the primary school: theory into practice
    1. Great Britain. Schools. Race relations
    I. Title II. Short, Geoffrey
    370.19'342'0941
    ISBN 0 7005 1196 2
    ISBN 0 7005 1197 0 (Pbk)

Typeset by David John Services Ltd., Slough, Berks.
Printed by Billing & Sons Ltd, Worcester

ISBN 0 7005 1196 2 (Hardback)
Code 8312 02 1

ISBN 0 7005 1197 0 (Paperback)
Code 8313 02 1

For our parents

Contents

Acknowledgements

We would like to thank a number of people for their advice and support during the writing of this book: Haydn Davies-Jones for reading and commenting constructively on the first draft; Lynn Herron for her excellent word-processing and administrative assistance; the staff and pupils at the various schools who made us welcome during the course of our research; Ian McDonough for the illustrations; and Barry Troyna with whom we have had many animated discussions! We are also grateful to Ian Florance (NFER–NELSON) for his many helpful suggestions.

Some of the ideas presented in this book were first developed in an article 'Breakthrough to political literacy', published in *Journal of Education Policy* in 1987. We would like to thank the publishers, Taylor and Francis, for allowing us to draw upon this material.

Finally, at a more personal level, Bruce Carrington would like to thank Liz, Alex and Rebecca who've had to put up with a lot.

Introduction

In recent years, there has been a tremendous growth in the literature on multicultural and antiracist education. This has been directed at both practising teachers and students on pre-service courses. The growth reflects the changing priorities of educational policy-makers especially since the urban disorders of 1980 and 1981, and the publication of the Rampton and Swann reports in 1981 and 1985. Although the expanding literature has served to highlight some of the dilemmas faced by practitioners, it may also have led many of them to perceive the issue as unduly esoteric, politically contentious and divorced from classroom reality. Teachers' resistance to these innovations may also be due partly to the failure of those concerned with the formation and implementation of policies in this area to provide unambiguous and workable strategies for implementation (Richards, 1986; Taylor, 1986). This criticism is not new as Peter Kowalczewski's appraisal of the debate on 'race' and education demonstrated in 1982. He argued that 'the teaching profession has tended to dismiss curriculum change in the area of multicultural education as irrelevant' and that the debate 'has left many teachers (and children) confused and perplexed' (Kowalczewski, 1982, p. 157).

Aware of these difficulties, our aim in writing this book is to provide teachers working in primary and middle schools with an accessible yet critical account of current initiatives to promote racial equality in and through education. To this end, we assess a range of teaching and organizational strategies held to be compatible with this goal and consider in particular the needs of the 'all white' school. To enable 'reflective teachers' (Pollard and Tann, 1987) concerned with the aims and consequences of their pedagogy (as well as with means and technical efficiency) to review and revise their own practice, we begin by appraising the main shifts in central and local government policy since the 1960s. We then consider the long standing debate between multiculturalists and antiracists and show that the two perspectives are not necessarily irreconcilable. An increasing number of educationalists have come to accept not only the need to combat racism in schools but that such measures are most likely to succeed if introduced at primary level. Endorsing the Swann Committee's (1985) view that teaching about 'race' should not be undertaken in isolation but rather should be tackled holistically (i.e., as part of a wider programme of political education), we consider the case for such initiatives in the primary school and examine the obstacles standing in their way. Particular attention is given to the claim that young children are both politically naive and innocent as well as intellectually incapable of coping with matters such as racism and sexism. To show that this claim has little or no foundation, we refer to the evidence on the development of children's political consciousness and understanding and the formation of various types of group identity.

Accepting the views of Her Majesty's Inspectorate that the curriculum should be applicable wherever possible to the pupils' own experience and lives (DES, 1985a), we argue .that teaching about 'taboo' and controversial subjects can be justified on the grounds of their relevance. It can also be justified on other, possibly more important, grounds. Attitudes and beliefs are shaped both directly and indirectly through the family, peer group, community and media, as well as through the school; they are 'caught' and 'taught'. In our view, the political and moral socialization of the young ought not to be left to chance. Schools, by making certain that controversial issues are dealt with in a detached and systematic manner (and particularly at a level appropriate to the children's abilities and aptitudes), can provide an invaluable counterbalance to other *ad hoc*, often overtly partisan and undesirable, agencies. Unless steps are taken in the primary school to develop children's capacity for critical and rational thinking, then folklore, playground gossip and other potentially malign and undemocratic influences may result in the failure of subsequent attempts to change their attitudes and beliefs. Engaging with the widespread and erroneous view that political educators are little more than left-wing subversives, we stress that political education (as currently conceived and practised) is strongly opposed to any form of indoctrination. On the contrary, it is predicated upon an unequivocal commitment to the principle of participatory democracy, open discussion and free access to information.

We demonstrate that although a considerable body of research on the development of group identities and preferences can be cited in support of antiracist and multicultural education, much of this work is not only dated but methodologically flawed and, on occasions, ethically suspect. Among other things, we draw attention to the mechanistic and artificial nature of many studies in this area and argue that researchers have often encouraged, reinforced and even forced their child subjects to employ racist frames of reference and articulate racist attitudes and beliefs. In addition, we show that the extant research focuses almost exclusively upon the affective rather than cognitive dimension of such attitudes and beliefs.

To redress the balance and surmount these difficulties, we present the findings of a recently completed ethnographic study. Based on semi-structured interviews with 161 children aged between 6 and 12, drawn from two 'all white' primary schools, the research explores the children's knowledge and understanding of 'race' together with gender and social class. This approach, we argue, can be more readily reconciled with our *holistic* priorities in teaching controversial issues. It is our contention that if such teaching is to be effective, then account must be taken of *inter alia* age-related differences in children's thinking about 'race' and other sociocultural and political phenomena.

Of course, additional factors must be examined when devising school-based initiatives in antiracist and multicultural education. In our view, it is imperative that consideration be given to the pupils' social and ethnic backgrounds and the location of their school, because manifestations of individual racism can vary both according to social class and locality (e.g., Husbands, 1983). Conscious of the dearth of literature on the 'all white' school, we draw upon our own case-study data to show how children from two schools – 'Oldtown Primary' and 'Denby Dock Middle' – respond to teaching about racism and other controversial issues. In the case study (and in the accompanying discussion of various organizational, curricular and pedagogical strategies) our aim is to address the practical difficulties which teachers encounter when planning and implementing policies to mitigate racial inequality and discrimination. If there is any readily discernible recurring theme running through our wide-ranging appraisal of these strategies, then it can best be summarized by Marshall McLuhan's (1964) well-known dictum: 'the medium is the message'. Throughout this and other parts of the book, we stress that if such policies are to have a lasting impact on pupils' attitudes and behaviour, then it will be necessary to take steps to democratize teaching and learning. In particular, the value of collaborative group work is underlined. Broadly speaking, we concur with the view that:

> The classroom should not be a threatening place dominated by authoritarian teachers, but a place in which children could feel confident in their relations with each other and with adults.
>
> (Richmond, 1985, p.224)

We recognize that teachers do not operate in a social and political vacuum and that schools cannot unilaterally change the social structure of which they are a part. For this reason, we focus on current controversies surrounding the role of the school in a multiracial and multicultural society. The lacunae of the Swann Report (1985) provide a point of departure. Amongst other things, the Report has been criticized for the inadequacy of its response to ethnic differences in attainment and for underplaying the extent to which racism may limit the attainment levels of black children. It has also been criticized for its failure to support both the legitimate demands of some minority groups for their own denominational schools and development of bilingual education. In relation to these issues, various questions are explored, including: What directions might further research on ethnic differences in attainment take? What are the implications of the apparent growth in demand for educational provision outside the mainstream among sections of the Afro-Caribbean and South Asian communities? Is there a conflict between antiracist and antisexist education; that is, do antiracists, by accepting the demands of some Muslim parents for single-sex, denominational schools, inhibit the emancipation of Muslim girls?

We conclude by considering the implications of our analysis for both initial and in-service teacher education. In making our recommendations, we are mindful of the range of constraints which currently impinge upon teachers and the attendant low morale within the profession. In 1981, the Rampton Report quoted one despondent teacher as saying: 'We have had mixed ability; we've gone Community and now it's bloody multicultural' (1981, p.29). We wonder what this teacher might say today with the continuing emphasis on accountability, the growth of centralism and the advent of the National Curriculum. Although the latter is not necessarily incompatible with the notion of antiracist and multicultural education, we nevertheless believe that the increased emphasis on 'the ideology of achievement' (see Burgess, 1988) does not augur well for such egalitarian measures. The form of pedagogy upon which the success of these measures depends is unlikely to flourish in a climate where undue emphasis is given to testing and assessment. Despite disclaimers to the contrary, the ethic of competitive individualism, so characteristic of our comprehensive schools (Hargreaves, 1982), will no doubt come to assume a higher profile in primary schools as well. As a result, the likelihood of experimentation and progressive innovation may well diminish with the increased emphasis on competition and the so-called 'core' subject areas. In the light of these changes, the fate of collaborative group work and other pedagogic strategies conducive to the development of empathy, cooperation, reciprocity and interdependence, remains to be seen.

1
'Race' and Schooling Policy: Old and New Orthodoxies

In Britain, in common with many other Western countries, the role of education in a multiracial and multiethnic society has been a matter of debate for more than two decades. Since the late 1970s, following the shift in educational policy from the goals of assimilation and integration, an increasing number of local authorities and individual schools have formulated policies in either multicultural education or, to a lesser degree, antiracist education. Responses to this development have been mixed, there has been greater support for such initiatives in multiracial rather than 'all white' schools, and in the maintained rather than the voluntary sector. Furthermore, the adoption of multicultural education has been considerably greater than its more radical and politically contentious counterpart, antiracism (Ball and Troyna, 1987; Troyna and Ball, 1985; Willey, 1984a). These initiatives, especially the latter, have been subjected to a barrage of criticism from the Right, where they have been variously disparaged as socially divisive, authoritarian and symptomatic of the 'new intolerance' (see Palmer, 1986). Sensational reporting in the media, particularly the tabloid press, has done little to inspire confidence among practitioners concerned with the implementation of these policies, or to allay the anxieties of parents. As we have argued elsewhere (Carrington and Short, 1989), the Association of London Authorities' (1987) leaflet, 'It's the Way That They Tell 'em', illustrates graphically the extent of this hostility towards the policies in question. Headlines referred to in the leaflet such as 'Race Spies Storm' (*Mail on Sunday*), 'Baa, Baa Green Sheep – Yes Green! – Sheep' (*Daily Mail*), and 'Loony Left in Wendy House

Row' (*Daily Express*) exemplify the way in which multicultural and antiracist education, together with other egalitarian measures, are frequently misrepresented, parodied and vilified by the media.

The primary concern of this chapter is to examine contemporary debates about 'race' and education. In order to place these debates into a wider context, we begin with a brief analysis of the main shifts in central and local government policy in this area during the post-war period. We then examine exemplars of multiculturalism and antiracism and compare and contrast their central theoretical tenets. Each of these diffuse educational ideologies will be critically appraised, and the claims of their respective advocates and detractors scrutinized. An attempt will be made to show that although some multiculturalists have come to accept the need for schools to address *directly* the issue of racism, and while there are antiracists who recognize the importance of teaching about cultural diversity, fundamental conceptual differences between the two perspectives continue to exist. Perhaps such differences are most apparent in the ways in which concepts such as 'racism' and 'culture' are handled. We hope to show, however, that these distinctions become increasingly more difficult to sustain at the level of pedagogical practice, where multiculturalists and antiracists alike would now appear to endorse various *common* strategies to 'combat racism' or 'reduce prejudice' as part of a wider programme of political or moral education (e.g., Short and Carrington, 1987; Troyna, 1987; Lynch, 1987).

Policy shifts: from assimilation to antiracism

As the work of various commentators has suggested, it is possible to discern a number of broad overlapping phases in British race and education policy (e.g., Street-Porter, 1978; Troyna, 1982; Brandt, 1986). These phases will be referred to as: (1) *laissez-faire*, (2) assimilation, (3) integration, (4) cultural pluralism, and (5) antiracism.

1   *Laissez-faire*

In education, as in other spheres, the political response to the presence of the ethnic minority groups during the post-war period prior to 1963 was essentially *laissez-faire*. Faced with labour short-ages in a number of sectors of the economy, politicians tended to underplay the social and cultural implications of immigration to Britain from the New Commonwealth countries. Undoubtedly, some took the unduly sanguine view that any form of coordinated policy was unnecessary because new migrants in the past had been assimilated within one or two generations; the racial discrimination and prejudice experienced by the newcomers from the West Indies, India and Pakistan was perceived as a temporary aberration, which would soon pass with their cultural absorption into a flexible and tolerant society. The 'race riots' which occurred in London and Nottingham in 1958 and the political furore to follow in their wake eventually brought the *laissez-faire* phase to an end. With the passing of the First Commonwealth Immigration Act in 1962, the state came to play an increasingly interventionist role in 'race relations' (Katznelson, 1973; Sivanandan, 1976).

2   Assimilation

From this juncture, various policies were implemented, directed towards the goal of assimilation. The key assumption which underpinned these interventions was that racial harmony largely depended upon the elimination of cultural barriers between the majority and minority populations. To fulfil this policy goal, the ethnic minorities were, in effect, called upon to suppress their own values and traditions. The implications of the policy for the education system were enunciated in the following unequivocal statement by the Commonwealth Immigrants Advisory Council in 1964:

> A national system of education must aim at producing citizens who can take their place in society properly equipped to exercise rights and perform duties the same as those of other citizens. If their parents were brought up in another culture and another tradition, children should be encouraged to respect it, but a national system cannot be expected to perpetuate the different values of immigrant children.
>
> (Cited in Kirp, 1979, pp. 45–6.)

Because policy-makers tended to perceive both linguistic diversity and the spatial concentration of ethnic minority pupils in some schools as major obstacles to assimilation, basic teaching provision in English as a second language (ESL) was introduced for South Asians and other bilingual pupils, along with the contentious and divisive practice of bussing.

The Local Government Act 1966 (section 11) provided local education authorities (LEAs) with some financial support towards the cost of hiring additional teachers and other staff required to deal with 'the presence within their areas of substantial numbers of immigrants whose language and customs are different from the rest of the community'. In general terms, bilingualism was not perceived as an asset, but rather was looked upon as an impediment to the educational progress of minority and majority pupils alike. As a result, the inclusion of non-European languages in the school curriculum was not encouraged. Furthermore, although South Asian and other bilingual pupils received some (albeit limited) ESL tuition, this facility was not extended to pupils from Afro-Caribbean backgrounds. According to Viv Edwards (1983), little account was taken of the linguistic needs of this latter group and, because of the paucity of initial and in-service training provision in the area, teachers were to remain largely ignorant about the differences between Creole dialects and standard English.

The second facet of the assimilation policy – bussing – was first outlined by the Department of Education and Science in June 1965. In its Circular 7/65, the DES called upon local authorities to disperse 'immigrant' pupils, asserting that if the proportion in any given school exceeded a third, then (p.4) 'serious strains emerge', 'problems become more difficult to solve' and 'the chance of assimilation becomes remote'. The circular attempted to allay the anxieties of some white parents by announcing measures to ensure that their children's progress would not be restricted by the (p. 8) 'undue preoccupation of teaching staff with the linguistic and other difficulties of other children'. The forced removal of South Asian and Afro-Caribbean children from their neighbourhood schools into schools in other parts of the local authority was also undertaken in the belief that it would result in them having greater contact with their white peers and the 'majority culture'. This intervention, as Carrington (1981) has argued elsewhere, was discriminatory both in its philosophy and consequences, for it reinforced the popular belief that such pupils constituted a problematic category in schools and concomitantly, singled them out (rather than whites) for 'dispersal'.

DES support for the measure ceased after 1971. The change in official attitude was brought about as a result of political pressures, on the one hand, and the abandonment of assimilation as the main policy goal, on the other. Despite the withdrawal of DES support and the recommendation of the Select Committee on Race Relations in 1973 that bussing should be phased out, it continued to be practised *openly* in some local authorities until its legality was eventually challenged in the courts, following an injunction taken out by the Race Relations Board in 1976 against the London Borough of Ealing. According to David Kirp (1979, p. 73), 'the racial explicitness of dispersal, essential to its operation, came to constitute the cause of its demise'.

3 Integration

After Roy Jenkins' influential speech (as Home Secretary in the Labour government) on 22 May 1966, an integrationist perspective, celebrating unity through diversity, eventually came to displace assimilation as the working paradigm of educational policy-makers. Jenkins described the new policy goal as 'not a flattening process of assimilation but as equal opportunity accompanied by cultural diversity in an atmosphere of mutual tolerance' (quoted in Rose *et al.*, 1969, p. 11). This 'vague prescription', as Barry Troyna and Jenny Williams (1986, p. 20) have argued, 'presaged changes more in political rhetoric than in practice'. Schools and LEAs were offered little guidance on the implementation of the policy, with the result that initiatives were undertaken on an *ad hoc* basis and largely confined to areas with Afro-Caribbean or South Asian populations. In general, these took the form of low-status additives to the existing curriculum (such as Black Studies in secondary schools) or other 'racially inexplicit' minimalist measures, which aimed, among other things, to bolster the self-esteem and group identity of ethnic minority pupils by making reference to their *supposed* lifestyles, histories and cultural traditions. The policy was also predicated upon an assumption that such modifications to the curriculum would, in turn, serve to reduce racial prejudice within the white population. Following the transition from assimilation to integration during the late 1960s, there was a proliferation of conferences and courses to inform teachers about the cultural backgrounds of ethnic minority children, life in India, Pakistan or the Caribbean, and the rudiments of the Hindu, Sikh and Muslim faiths (e.g., Street-Porter, 1978; Bolton, 1979). The continued focus during the integrationist phase on the inhibiting effects of actual (or imagined) cultural differences, coupled with the 'folkloric' preoccupation of schools with the feasts, customs, festivals and food of 'immigrants' (Lynch, 1986a, p. 46), served to reinforce inaccurate and often pejorative stereotypes of Afro-Caribbeans and South Asians and, moreover, gave credence to the widespread perception of these groups as 'aliens' or 'outsiders'.

As well as these minor concessions to cultural diversity, various projects were launched from 1968 onwards to tackle the problems of urban disadvantage. The Home Office's Urban Aid programme and the DES' Educational Priority Area (EPA) action-research project were the precursors of a number of related interventions, set up by both Labour and Conservative governments, ostensibly to interrupt the so-called 'cycle of deprivation' (Community Development Project, 1977). Neither the Urban Aid programme nor the EPA project was, in the words of David Kirp (1979) 'racially explicit': that is, intended to obviate racial inequality and discrimination *per se*. Both interventions, in common with others which followed in their wake, were aimed at the 'disadvantaged' in general. For example, the purpose of urban aid was to initiate a programme of expenditure mainly on education, housing, health and social welfare in 'areas of special need'. The Home Office, in its Circular 1/1968, defined these areas in terms of multiple criteria: that is, inferior housing conditions, high levels of unemployment and juvenile crime, large families and an 'immigrant' population. The EPA project was also universalistic in its orientation: the five urban areas in which this experiment in 'compensatory education' was conducted, were designated on the basis of criteria for educational disadvantage laid down in the Plowden Report (i.e., low socioeconomic status of parents, poor amenities in the home, high teacher and pupil turnover, significant proportion of 'immigrants', etc.). The programme of 'positive discrimination' implemented during the experiment did not single out black children as having specific educational needs (and therefore warranting differential treatment) but rather equated their needs with those of their white working-class peers (Carrington, 1981).

Despite the growing concern within the Afro-Caribbean community about the low attainment levels of black children and their apparent overrepresentation and misplacement in schools for the educationally subnormal (Tomlinson, 1982; Coard, 1971), the DES continued to resist pressures to implement specific measures to promote racial equality in schools. Instead, it reiterated the view that the educational needs of ethnic minority children were essentially no different from those of other sections of the population. With race and ethnicity not forming the basis of any grant which it made, the DES could readily justify its decision in 1972 to cease the publication of statistical data on such differences. In 1973, when the Select Committee on Race Relations and Immigration recommended that a separate fund be established to enable local authorities to meet the 'special educational needs of ethnic minority groups' (House of Commons, 1973), the DES responded with an outright rejection of the proposal and, in the following year, proceeded to establish a generic Educational Disadvantage Unit within the Department, and an independent Centre for Advice and Information on Educational Disadvantage. The Select Committee restated its recommendation in a report on the West Indian Community in 1977 which, among other things, sought to highlight the widespread concern about 'the poor performance of West Indian children in school'. It proposed that, 'as a matter of urgency, the Government should institute a high level and independent inquiry into the causes of the underachievement of children of West Indian origin in maintained schools and the remedial action required' (House of Commons, 1977, para. 57). Although the request for a special fund was again rebuffed, the DES did eventually establish a Committee of Inquiry in March 1979. The Committee, which in the first instance was chaired by Anthony Rampton, was asked 'to review the educational needs and attainments of children from ethnic minority groups' giving 'early and particular attention to the educational needs and attainments of pupils of West Indian origin' (1981, p. 1).

4   Cultural pluralism

During the late 1970s and early 1980s, it is possible to discern yet another shift in the debate on the role of the school in a multiracial, multiethnic society. For example, in 1977 the Inner London Education Authority became the first of many LEAs to produce policy statements endorsing a cultural pluralist perspective. However, most of these did not take any decisive action in this sphere until after the urban disorders in St Paul's, Brixton, Toxteth, Handsworth and other centres in 1980 and 1981 (e.g., Mullard *et al.*, 1983; Troyna, 1985). At the central government level, the Green Paper *Education and Schools* (DES, 1977) can be regarded as the harbinger of a change in official attitude. It argued that since 'our society is a multicultural, multiracial one... the curriculum should reflect a sympathetic understanding of different cultures and races' (p. 41). By 1981, as Maurice Craft (1984) has indicated, multicultural education was to become 'the focus of educational debate', when no less than four major reports on the subject appeared. Of these, the report of the Rampton Committee was undoubtedly the most influential, despite the controversy surrounding its publication. Eschewing the *ad hoc* incremental approaches to curricular change characteristic of interventions directed towards integration, the Committee called for a systematic review of the curriculum in every school, irrespective of its ethnic composition.

> We believe that a curriculum which takes account of the multiracial nature of society is needed for all schools, not just those in which there are ethnic minority pupils... It is important to make it clear that a curriculum that reflects the multiracial nature of society should not be seen as something different or extra to be added on to the existing curriculum of a school.
>
> (Rampton Report, 1981, pp. 28–9)

Advocating a positive approach to cultural difference and stressing the need to combat curricular ethnocentrism, the Committee (p. 27) contended that:

> A 'good' education should enable a child to understand his [*sic*] own society, and to know enough about other societies to enhance that understanding. A 'good' education cannot be based on one culture only, and in Britain where ethnic minorities form a permanent and integral part of the population, we do not believe that education should seek to iron out the differences between cultures, nor attempt to draw everyone into the dominant culture. On the contrary, it will draw upon the experiences of the many cultures that make up our society and thus broaden the cultural horizons of every child. That is what we mean by 'multicultural' education.

The first of Alan Little and Richard Willey's (1981) reports for the now-defunct Schools Council (published in the same year as the Rampton Report) revealed a considerable gap between the pluralist policy and LEA and school practice. Their survey of provision, the first of its kind for nearly a decade, was based upon a national sample of some 525 secondary schools and 70 local authorities. Among other things, they reported that whereas few schools in multiracial areas had undertaken a systematic review of their teaching, many had come to accept the view that 'an awareness of Britain's multiethnic society should permeate the curriculum as a whole', and recognize that 'the insertion of additives such as Black Studies' was antipathetical to the goal of cultural pluralism (Little and Willey, 1981, p. 20). Although the survey revealed that professional attitudes towards this policy were generally positive in multiracial areas, the prevalent view in areas with few or no ethnic minority pupils was that 'the wider ethnic composition of society has little relevance for their schools'. (As we show in Chapter 7, there are indications that teachers in such areas continue to view these developments in educational policy largely with indifference or even hostility.) In their conclusions, Little and Willey were critical of several organizations, including the DES, local authorities, examination boards and teacher education institutions, for their failure to give 'clear guidance' on the ways the policy objectives can be achieved.

During the period from 1981 to 1985, various attempts were made to surmount these difficulties. For example, the Schools Council, as James Lynch has pointed out, 'took a lead in requesting all its subject boards to scrutinise their work in the context of a multicultural society' (Lynch, 1986a, p. 51). Initiatives were also taken to improve the quality of this aspect of teacher education: the national programme, 'Training the Trainers' was launched in late 1982 with a view to providing staff in teacher education with the opportunity to extend their knowledge of multicultural education and to reappraise their institution's response to cultural pluralism. By 1984, both the Council for the Accreditation of Teacher Education and the pressure group NAME (then the National Association for Multiracial Education) had produced guidelines for the reform of teacher education (Lynch, 1986b). In the following year, the final report of the Committee of Inquiry into the Education of Children from Ethnic Minority Groups (then chaired by Lord Swann) eventually appeared. The report, *Education for All*, was to provide further impetus to the development of multicultural education, particularly in 'all white' areas. Lord Swann and his colleagues gave the following unequivocal support to the ideology of pluralism:

> We consider that a multiracial society such as ours would in fact function most effectively and harmoniously on the basis of pluralism which enables, expects and encourages members of all ethnic groups, both minority and majority, to participate fully in shaping the society as a whole within a framework of commonly accepted values, practices and procedures, whilst also allowing and, where necessary, assisting the ethnic minority communities in maintaining their distinct ethnic identities within this common framework. Clearly the balance between the shared common identity of society as a whole and the distinct identities of different ethnic groups is crucial in establishing and maintaining a pluralist society, and it must be recognised that such a society places obligations on both the minority and majority groups within it, if it is to offer them a full range of benefits and opportunities.
>
> (Swann Report, 1985, p. 5).

The Committee outlined various measures to celebrate cultural diversity in the curriculum and counter stereotyping. (We discuss these measures in greater detail in Chapter 5.) As well as urging that all schools offer their pupils 'a full and balanced education' which incorporates a 'global perspective', Lord Swann and his colleagues also stressed that 'the issue of racism at both institutional and individual level should be considered openly and efforts made to counter it' (1985, p. 329). According to the Committee, such teaching could be undertaken as part of a wider programme of political education.

5 Antiracism

In making this recommendation, the Swann Committee were no doubt acknowledging some of the criticisms which had been levelled by antiracists against multicultural education throughout the early 1980s and before. The critique took various forms: some commentators, such as Maureen Stone (1981), were to disparage multicultural education as a form of compensatory education based upon mistaken assumptions about 'the poor, negative self-concept' of black children; others merely dismissed it as a social control technique employed by schools to curb the growth of black disaffection (e.g., Mullard, 1982). The emphasis of multicultural education on cultural differences (actual or apparent), rather than racism and racial inequality, was also to become a cause for concern, as David Milner's pithy remarks in 1982 suggest:

> To paraphrase Goering, when I hear the word 'multicultural', I reach for my spear. It was not always so, but in the last few years the term has been used to denote so many different philosophies and practices that it no longer has any precise meaning; worse, it has been used as a synonym for multiracial education, which has had the effect of diverting attention away from the more important implications of that term. When, in the mid-1970s, a number of people argued for multicultural, multiracial education, they were quite clear that the two components should be inseparable. Then, as now, it was, in my view, meaningless to discuss black (or brown) minorities and their relationship to the white majority in purely cultural terms. British society did not consign black people to its bargain basement because of their dress, diet or unfamiliar customs, it did so because of their race.
>
> (Milner, 1982, p.72)

Subsequently, this line of argument has been extended by various commentators critical of the racially inexplicit and apolitical nature of many current, pluralist initiatives in education. It is to this debate that we now turn.

Antiracist education versus multicultural education

Both antiracism and multiculturalism can be seen as diffuse educational ideologies which have given rise to a wide range of interpretations and practices. While we accept that it may not always be possible to draw hard and fast distinctions between these two perspectives, they can, nevertheless, be seen as differing in their operational concepts and educational concerns. We will attempt to adumbrate these differences.

Although many multiculturalists in recent years have sought to incorporate some aspects of antiracism in their approaches (cf.

Swann Report, 1985; Banks, 1986; Lynch, 1987), it has been argued that a gulf between the two perspectives remains. For example, as Barry Troyna and Jenny Williams have attempted to show, the starting point of multicultural education is the individual rather than institutions or the social structure (e.g., Troyna and Williams, 1986, pp. 44–59). The goal of multicultural education is to foster mutual understanding and tolerance by changing the perceptions and attitudes of individuals through a pluralist programme of curricular reform. The sympathetic portrayal of a range of cultures and lifestyles in the curriculum is seen as benefiting all pupils, irrespective of their background. In the case of ethnic minorities, it is held that this will lead to enhanced self-esteem and, concomitantly, an improvement in academic attainment and increased opportunities in the labour market; with white pupils, such measures are seen as being conducive to 'prejudice reduction'. In contrast, antiracists are primarily concerned with differences in life chances rather than lifestyles and, in particular, the structural basis of racism and racial inequality in schools and society at large. As well as calling for changes in the formal curriculum to include teaching about racism and racial discrimination as part of a wider programme of political education, antiracists advocate a systematic appraisal of the hidden curriculum to redress racial inequalities in *inter alia* staffing, assessment and grouping procedures. While Troyna (1987) has continued to stress that the ideologies in question remain 'irreconcilable', the impact of antiracist education on multicultural education should not be underestimated. As James Lynch, one of the UK's leading exponents of multiculturalism, has recently pointed out:

> The radical antiracist critique has led to a number of positive developments in multicultural education, such as: increased analysis of the social context; renewed focus on the needs of all children; acceptance of the need for educational responses to structural and personal racism; recognition of the need for greater dialogue and potent participation of all cultural groups; new policies and delivery strategies to outlaw racism; increased focus on the role of the school in prejudice reduction; reform of curricula, assessment and organisation to eradicate racist policies and procedures.
>
> (Lynch, 1987, pp. 9–10)

Despite this change in emphasis, antiracists have neverthele extended their critique to Lynch, the Swann Committee and othei proponents of what Richard Hatcher (1987a) has described as the 'new multiculturalism'. Let us consider their objections to multicultural education in more detail.

As Troyna (1987) has attempted to show, much of what passes for multicultural education is based upon various dubious assumptions about, for example, the apparent influence of curricular ethnocentrism on the educational performance of black pupils or on the racial attitudes of whites. In the case of the latter, he cites the research of Connor (1972) to argue that attempts to increase pupils' awareness of other cultures do not necessarily result in them showing greater tolerance: indeed, such interventions are just as likely to have the opposite effect (by reinforcing in-group identification and solidarity). Notwithstanding this, as we have indicated elsewhere (Short and Carrington, 1987), there are grounds for arguing that unless a concerted and systematic attempt is made by schools to extend pupils' knowledge of cultural differences, any erroneous beliefs and misconceptions which they may already hold about other groups will simply go unchallenged. While we are not endorsing the simplistic view that individual racism can always be countered by appeal to reason or truth (Jones, 1985), we are arguing that unless such beliefs are challenged early on, they could develop into something far more serious.

Culture and power

Of course, in making this observation, we recognize that multiculturalists' attempts to represent cultural diversity in the curriculum have, on occasions, led to ethnic minority cultures being caricatured, stereotyped and depicted as exotica. As David Milner (1983), among others, has indicated, there is often a wide discrepancy between ethnic minority groups' lifestyles and cultural traditions as *represented* in the curriculum and the *actual conditions of existence* of these groups in Britain today. In Milner's view, the multiculturalist is invariably faced with these dilemmas:

How do we convey diversity within cultures in simple terms, and how do we avoid the opposite extreme of stereotyping? How would a Venusian multiculturalist design a curriculum to reflect the culture of new British immigrants? Roast beef, Vaughan Williams, morris dancing and religious observance (with some 'dialect' lessons in Standard English). Or fish and chips, Tom Jones, disco, and church attendance three times per life per capita, all lessons to be conducted in Cockney or Scouse dialects? The point is not a facetious one, for what we actually do under the banner of multiculturalism may get perilously close to this kind of pastiche.

(Milner, 1983, pp. 225–6)

More recently, Judyth Sachs (1986), in an appraisal of developments in multicultural education in Australia, Britain and elsewhere, has argued that the often narrow focus on the 'more obvious or exotic' facets of the lifestyles of a variety of ethnic groups, can (in part) be attributed to the failure of educationalists and policy-makers to take cognisance of current sociological and anthropological approaches to culture. She argues that multiculturalists have tended to operate with 'naive and outdated conceptions of culture'. Such conceptions are often static and apolitical, and take little or no account of the extent to which the lifestyles of individuals and groups reflect their life chances. In Sachs' view, culture must be viewed as more than the heritage (i.e. traditions, history, language, arts, religion, customs, values, etc.) and material artefacts of a group of people. Rather, it must be seen as a form of 'knowledge' which members of a group draw upon to interpret their day-to-day experiences and to make sense of their lives. Sachs shows that the undue emphasis given to the 'odd and bizarre' aspects of other cultures in multicultural education not only serves to accentuate the differences between groups (thereby creating or reinforcing stereotypes), it may also lead to 'crucial issues' such as power, conflict, lack of access to social and economic resources and racism being ignored.

Other commentators have also drawn attention to the deficiencies of multiculturalists' attempts to conceptualize culture. Hatcher (1987a, p. 188), for example, argued that

[although] culture is the central concept around which the new multiculturalism is constructed, the concept is given only a taken-for-granted commonsense meaning, impoverished both theoretically and in terms of concrete lived experience. It is a concept of culture innocent of class.

In his view, multiculturalists, such as Banks and Lynch have generally failed to acknowledge the central influence of social class on 'individual subjectivities' and, in differentially shaping attitudes, beliefs and patterns of behaviour. His analysis suggests that curricular initiatives to combat racism must not only take account of pupils' social backgrounds, but must also engage with the *particular forms* taken by racism within their culture and locality.

The research of Christopher Husbands (1983) into factors underlying urban support for the National Front (NF) can be cited to corroborate this claim. His survey into the political and racial attitudes of a sample of 1500 white adults (drawn from ten urban areas in England) revealed that although hostility towards black people was not confined to any one social class, 'racism in the working class ... takes specific forms and is based upon concerns that differentiate it from the phenomenon as found in other social classes' (p. 142). His data show how these forms can vary from place to place. For example, black people were more likely to be blamed for declining opportunities in the labour market in Hackney, Lewisham, Leicester or Slough than in Wolverhampton or Blackburn. Similarly, whereas local-area deterioration was frequently attributed to the presence of black people in Leicester, Slough and Bradford, this form of racial scapegoating was far less prevalent among those respondents living in Hackney or Charnwood.

Racism and educationalists

The critics of the new multiculturalism have not only highlighted the deficiencies of its approach to culture, but have also argued that its approach to racism is similarly lacking. Not surprisingly, much (though by no means all) of this criticism has been directed towards the Swann Report. The critique has focused on a number of issues, including: the ambiguous nature of Swann's operationalization of racism; the tendency of the Report to conflate racism with prejudice; and its failure to examine the phenomenon in the context of wider political and economic processes.

As Sheila Patterson (1985) has shown, the concept of racism employed by Swann is not only unwieldy and unhelpful to practitioners, but also serves to reinforce the simplistic view that 'racial discrimination is the direct outcome of racially prejudiced attitudes'. In her view:

> The concept is not used in its original sense of a doctrine which maintains that racial and cultural traits are connected and that some races are inherently superior to others (cf., *Dictionary of the Social Sciences*), but in the currently modish sense, as a shorthand to cover any manifestation of majority beliefs, attitudes or behaviour that can even remotely be linked with the terms 'race', 'racial' or even 'ethnic'.
>
> (Patterson, 1985, p. 242)

Numerous examples are culled from the Report to illustrate the point. Patterson shows how racism is variously depicted as: 'prejudiced attitudes and behaviour, arising from historical and other negative stereotypes about non-white minorities', and 'the negative prejudice that sees ethnic minority groups, even when long settled as "outsiders", "strangers", "immigrants", "foreigners"' (p. 242). She also draws attention to the many disparate examples of 'racism in practice' provided in the Report. These include teachers' attitudes and behaviour towards ethnic minority pupils; manifestations of racial harassment and violence; and institutional racism (defined as 'a range of long-established systems, practices and procedures devised to meet the needs of a relatively homogeneous society' (p. 243)).

Subsequently, Bob Carter and Jenny Williams (1987) have been among those who have raised similar objections to the Swann Committee's response to racism. They argue that racism is 'primarily presented as individual prejudice, based on negative cultural stereotypes' (p. 172), and go on to castigate the Committee for its failure to set the phenomenon 'within any model of structural inequality'. Their critique is of particular interest because it also draws attention to the limitations of many antiracists' approaches, especially those based on the formula 'racism = power + prejudice'. According to Carter and Williams, this formula, which underpins the widespread and controversial Racism Awareness Training courses and some LEA policy statements, rests upon a number of untenable assumptions: power in British society is in the hands of white people; as a consequence of colonialism (which has left an indelible mark on their consciousness) only white people can be racist; and all white people (including antiracists and others who do not consciously hold racist attitudes) cannot escape the influence of racism because institutional practices and procedures are loaded in their favour. Moreover, they argue that this approach to racism 'rests on a personalised view of power and an understanding of racism which sets it aside from economic relations'. As a result of this, 'white power and white attitudes within particular institutions become the focus of policies' (Carter and Williams, 1987, p. 174).

Before moving on to examine Carter and Williams' alternative conceptualization of racism, it should be noted that the formula 'racism = power + prejudice' has also been criticized along much the same lines by commentators of the New Right. The essay collection, edited by Frank Palmer (1986), *Antiracism: An Assault on Education and Value* (which includes contributions by Anthony Flew, Roger Scruton, Caroline Cox, David Levy, Ray Honeyford and John Marks), may be regarded as exemplary of this position.

Leaving aside the crude and misleading depiction of antiracism as a form of indoctrination and political propaganda, let us examine briefly some of the observations made in this book about the current usage of the term 'racism' in education. We will focus on the work of John Marks, as it is particularly germane.

Marks (1986, p. 33), in common with Patterson, and Carter and Williams, begins by arguing that 'shifting and imprecise definitions of "racism" are perhaps the most important sources of confusion and conflict'. He then proceeds to question the so-called 'composite' definition of racism employed by ILEA and Berkshire Education Committee in their respective policy statements of 1983. The following (identical) operationalization of racism was given in both statements:

> There are certain routine practices, customs and procedures in our society whose consequence is that black people have poorer jobs, health, housing and life-chances than do the majority... These practices and customs are maintained by relations and structures of power, and are justified by centuries-old beliefs and attitudes which hold that black people are inherently inferior to white people – biologically, culturally or both. 'Racism' is a shorthand

term for this combination of discriminatory practices; unequal relations and structures of power; and negative beliefs and attitudes.

(Marks, 1986, p. 34)

In Marks' view, the use of such a diffuse definition of racism not only 'makes it almost impossible to argue clearly and rationally about racial questions', but it also supports the view that 'in Britain today, only white people are capable of "racism"' (p. 34).

In contrast to Marks and his associates, Carter and Williams (though critical of aspects of antiracist education as currently conceived and practised) are nevertheless supportive of the innovation. Few would take issue with Carter and Williams' view that if racism in education is to be 'the focus of analysis and reforming policies', then its meaning must be clear and unambiguous. It is their contention that racism must be reconceptualized as follows:

The core of racism is the assignment of characteristics in a deterministic way to a group, or groups, of persons. These characteristics are usually articulated around some cultural or biological feature such as skin colour or religion; they are regarded as inherent and unalterable precisely because they are seen as derived from one's 'race'. 'Race-ism' then employs these 'race-ial' characteristics to explain behaviour, feelings, attitudes and ways of life. It is important to recognise that 'race-ism' does not rest on the objective fact of 'race'. 'Races' cannot be said to exist in any valid biological sense; they are socially constructed. Groups of people become racialised, defined as a 'race'. They are held to possess certain unchangeable characteristics which are constitutive of their 'race'. 'Race' is therefore constructed through a process of ascription. An attribute (skin colour, religion, country of origin, language) becomes the basis of an individual's identity. It is thus considered to be an unalterable feature of those human beings so defined: for example, greed comes to be regarded as an aspect of 'Jewish-ness'; criminality comes to be regarded as an aspect of 'West Indian-ness'.

Racism is therefore more than the sum of individual prejudice: it becomes an organising principle of popular consciousness.

(Carter and Williams, 1987, pp. 176–7)

Having clarified the meaning of racism, Carter and Williams then examine the implications of their analysis for educational research and policy on racial inequality. Among other things, they call for the abandonment of the use of 'oversimplified' categories such as 'Afro-Caribbean', 'Asian' and 'White'. Along with other authors (e.g., Troyna, 1984), they argue that when comparisons are made between such heterogeneous groupings (for example, in relation to differences in attainment, or in the selection and allocation of pupils to sets, bands or streams), appropriate account must be taken of other salient variables, *including* social class, gender and age. We discuss these issues at greater length in Chapters 5 and 6.) They are especially critical of policies which incorporate 'vague exhortations to abolish institutional racism', or 'which assume that no change will occur until the attitudes of the majority of teachers are altered' (p. 180). Although they call for the development of policies which focus upon *discriminatory behaviour*, they recognize that difficulties are likely to be encountered when such policies are implemented and monitored.

Reconciling the irreconcilable

Although multiculturalists and antiracists continue to differ in their operational concepts and educational concerns, the gulf between them is no longer as 'deep and as wide as the Grand Canyon'. Indeed, there would appear to be some degree of congruence between the two perspectives *at the level of practice*, where similar (and, on occasions, identical) pedagogical and organizational strategies are now espoused. It is to this development that we now turn.

In his recent book, *Prejudice Reduction and the Schools* (1987), James Lynch has argued that teachers in Western democracies have a crucial role to play in prejudice reduction. According to Lynch, it is 'the teachers' task to morally empower their pupils to discard existing prejudices and to resist the absorption of new ones, and to enable pupils to become morally autonomous as well as socially responsible' (p. xii). With this and related goals in mind, he continues to stress the importance of a pluralist approach to the curriculum (cf., Lynch, 1983, 1986a). In addition, he recommends various other measures to democratize teaching and learning, promote collegiality and foster improved communication between the home and the school. It is Lynch's contention that if schools are to combat 'prejudice' in its 'many forms' (i.e., 'racism', 'sexism', 'classism' and 'credism'), then steps must be taken to create a school ethos which 'espouses democratic cultural pluralism, in its values and actions'. Among other things, he calls for 'pedagogical strategies to boost pupils' locus of control' (Lynch, 1987, p. 21) and urges teachers to experiment with techniques such as 'peer-tutoring' and 'collaborative group work', which can help to foster interdependence, cooperation and reciprocity. As well as these strategies, he also advocates that particular attention is given to the discussion of moral issues and dilemmas in the curriculum, and that role play and simulation exercises are also employed to broach such issues; direct teaching is recommended for 'correcting misinformation' and challenging stereotypes. Emphasizing the need for a holistic approach to 'prejudice reduction', Lynch outlines a number of organizational strategies for combating discriminatory attitudes and behaviour and for promoting greater equality of opportunity. Following Banks (1985), he contends that any effective policy in this area must be directed towards 'institutional reform of the whole school', since 'hidden values have a more cogent impact on pupils' attitudes than the formal programme of studies' (p. 60). Such a policy would focus on various facets of school life, including staffing composition and staff development; examinations, assessment and testing; procedures for dealing with 'prejudiced behaviour'; rules and regulations governing areas of the curriculum such as religious education, physical education and craft design technology, 'where issues of racism, credism or sexism are likely to arise'; language provision, especially for bilingual and multilingual pupils and their parents; and issues relating to parental and community participation.

Although rejecting Lynch's conflation of racism with individual prejudice and his sanguine view that racist beliefs can be dislodged simply through dialogue and appeal to reason (Hatcher, 1987a), antiracists have nevertheless endorsed many comparable strategies for intervention. As we have indicated elsewhere (Carrington and Short, 1987; Carrington and Troyna, 1988), antiracist education may be regarded as a constituent of a wider programme of political education which seeks to extend participation in the democratic process by equipping young people with the range of skills and dispositions needed to become decent, fairminded, responsible and informed citizens. This approach aims to develop their political (and moral) autonomy by encouraging them to take a critical stance towards ideological information; give reasons in support of a point of view; be open-minded and show respect for evidence; act with empathy and humanitarianism; explore fundamental questions relating to social justice, equality and human rights; and extend their appreciation of how power is exercised (and by whom) in our society. As such, it may provide an *appropriate* context for young people to appraise their own (and others) taken for granted beliefs and assumptions about 'race' and other political issues. In common with multiculturalists such as Lynch and other commentators who identify themselves more closely with an antiracist position (e.g., Brandt, 1986), we have suggested that such a programme would invariably necessitate a restructuring of relationships in many schools and classrooms. For example, we have argued that an authoritarian environment (where didacticism prevails and where hierarchy, competition and individualism are revered), is less conducive to the development of pupils' political and moral autonomy than a democratic one, stressing participation, cooperation and collaboration. As we indicate in Chapter 5, there is considerable research evidence from the United States and Britain (e.g., King, 1986; Yeomans, 1983) to show that collaborative learning not only serves to heighten young people's social awareness and interpersonal skills and improve inter-ethnic relations within the school, but does so without any apparent adverse effect on their attainment. Indeed, under certain conditions, levels of attainment may actually improve. Because antiracist education embraces teaching and learning strategies which have the potential to enhance the cognitive, social and affective development of children, we would maintain – contrary to the disclaimers of some critics on the Right – that it is entirely compatible with a 'good' or 'effective' education.

A cursory examination of other facets of contemporary antiracist practice would appear to lend support to Mal Leicester's claim that 'a fake dichotomy is implicit in much of the present debate' (1986, p. 7). For example, Lynch's observations about the need for 'holistic institutional policies' to tackle racial and other forms of inequality, or his deliberations about the importance of actively involving parents in the formation, implementation and monitoring of such policies, have also been echoed by antiracists (e.g., Campbell, 1986).

Similarly, as we have already indicated, multiculturalists have come to acknowledge the need for all schools, *irrespective of phase or ethnic composition*, to teach about the origins and manifestations of racism as part of a wider programme of political education. According to the Swann Committee:

> All schools should be offering their pupils as part of a 'good' education the ability to accept a range of differing and possibly conflicting points of view and to argue rationally and independently about the principles which underlie these, free from preconceived prejudices or stereotypes, and to recognise and resist false arguments and propaganda – as in a sense 'political' skills. We believe that effective political education must help pupils to appreciate the contribution which they as individuals can make to the decision-making process at various levels. Effective political education should also lead youngsters to consider fundamental issues such as social justice and equality and this should in turn cause them to reflect on the origins and mechanisms of racism and prejudice at an individual level.
>
> Some educationists have argued that school pupils are insufficiently mature and responsible to be able to comprehend politically sensitive issues such as racism and to cope with them in a balanced and rational manner. Even primary-age pupils however have views and opinions on various 'political' issues and are subject to a range of overt and covert political influences based on values and assumptions from their homes, their peers and the media.
>
> (Swann Report, 1985, pp. 335–6)

Perhaps, in view of such developments, a case can be made for abandoning the distinction between antiracism and multiculturalism altogether.

Summary

In this chapter, we have delineated the major changes in the debate about race and education in post-war Britain. We have argued that although antiracists and multiculturalists may continue to draw on differing conceptual frameworks, a convergence between the two perspectives would seem to be taking place at the level of practice, where largely compatible pedagogical, organizational and curricular strategies are currently being advocated. There would now appear to be some agreement among educationalists that teaching about racism (and other contentious issues) should begin in the primary school. In the next chapter, we examine the basis of this claim.

2
Education for Participatory Democracy

Because of the links between 'race' and power, we have argued that any curricular initiative in antiracist/multicultural education (AME) should form part of a wider programme of political and moral education directed towards the goal of participatory democracy. In this chapter, we focus on the primary school and attempt to show that teachers in this sector have a crucial and legitimate role to play in developing their pupils' understanding of a range of controversial issues, especially racism, sexism and other types of discrimination. We begin by examining teachers', parents' and politicians' resistance to the notion of political education in the primary school and by engaging with populist perceptions and misconceptions of innovation in this sphere. Following a discussion of these and other constraints, including legislation, which currently militate against such teaching, we then make the case for political education at this level, by drawing upon the extant research on children's political consciousness and socialization and on the development of various forms of collective identity and awareness. We conclude by appraising a number of methods for dealing with the controversial issues in the classroom, including the so-called 'neutral-chair' approach.

Political education and the primary school

Despite the continuing opposition to political education from various quarters and the apparently widespread perception in Britain that politics has 'little to do with childhood', political education is nevertheless included in the formal curriculum of an increasing number of secondary schools, either as a subject in its own right, or as an aspect of 'personal and social education', 'social studies', 'social and life skills' or the Technical and Vocational Educational Initiative (TVEI) (Harber, 1987; Stradling *et al.*, 1984). Secondary teachers would appear to be more amenable to political education than their primary colleagues, who, according to Alistair Ross (1984, p. 131) generally view the 'harsh realities' of politics as having 'no place in the comfortable world that their primary schools propagate to children'. In accounting for the minimal impact of political education at this level, Doug Harwood (1985) has suggested that teachers not only tend to have an 'inadequate grasp of its aim and objectives', but may also be inclined 'to underestimate their pupils' degree of political sophistication and knowledge'.

This view has also been endorsed by Robin Alexander (1984), whose work suggests that the continuing influence of Piagetian psychology and idealist conceptions of 'childhood innocence' may prompt primary teachers to argue that contentious issues such as racism, sexism, unemployment and international conflicts should not be dealt with in the primary curriculum. As well as claiming that such issues are largely beyond the grasp of those of primary school age, it is Alexander's view that some teachers will 'argue in accordance with the "cocoon" principle, that young children's security should not be disturbed by confronting them with issues that the mature adult has difficulty in coping with' (p. 34). Sometimes staff will go to great lengths to avoid certain 'taboo' subjects such as 'race' or 'death'. For example, Dunn's (1986) reflections on his experiences as an INSET evaluator show that there may be a tendency for primary teachers to ignore or underestimate the influence of racism and prejudice on younger children, and for staff in this sector to show a reluctance to discuss 'anything to do with race in their classrooms' (p. 188). The same may also be true of 'death', as King's (1978) case study of infant schools has suggested. In this, an incident is described in which teachers are observed removing a sick guinea pig from a classroom so as to prevent the children witnessing (and having to reconcile themselves with) the animal's death. It is hardly surprising, in view of these attitudes and beliefs, that political education at this level is perceived as inappropriate, or even as 'beyond the pale'.

Teaching controversial and 'taboo' issues

In the present political environment, it is unlikely that such attitudes and beliefs will easily be dislodged. Leaving aside the question 'What controversial issues ought to be examined in the curriculum and when should teaching begin?', the frequent allegations in the national media and political fora about bias and indoctrination in schools have served to reinforce opposition to political education both within and outside the teaching profession. Together with initiatives in AME, peace studies and sex education, political education has been the subject of extensive criticism and vilification. Although media attention (and disapprobation) has largely focused on the policies of Labour-controlled metropolitan local authorities such as ILEA, Haringey and Brent, as Steve Brigley, Peter Coates and Homer Noble (1988, p. 50) have recently pointed out:

> Little notice has been taken of the fact that similar problems with controversial and 'taboo' issues may occur as frequently in rural areas; in fact many schools cope with such issues as part of their daily routine.

To illustrate this point, they go on to describe several disputes: a row over 'the alleged harmful effects of teaching about the occult' in an Okehampton school; an attempt by local politicians in the same county to prevent the use of lapel badges and car stickers by teachers that 'promote any cause which might be deemed political'; and a conflict between parents and a school about a course planned for 12- and 13-year-olds on 'friendship and cooperation' which dealt, among other things, with prejudice against homosexuals. Brigley and colleagues claim that teachers in rural areas who elect to teach about such issues often have to do so without the institutional backing of their school or local authority. As a result of their greater vulnerability to external pressures (as compared, for example, with their counterparts in Haringey), many 'err on the side of caution', and avoid making any reference to a potentially controversial or 'taboo' topic in their teaching. Paradoxically, this form of self-censorship, or flaccid non-partisanship, is a form of bias *per se*. To take such a stance is not only anathema to good education, it is also at variance with the principle of democracy itself, because misconceptions and misinformation go uncorrected, and bigotry and intolerance are allowed to pass largely without comment.

There is, of course, no unanimity about what constitutes a 'controversial' or 'taboo' issue. As the above study illustrates, there may be widespread spatial variations in what both teachers and parents regard as an issue compatible with established norms and values. Political allegiance, ethnic and religious affiliation and the age of the pupils concerned will also have a bearing upon what is deemed appropriate and acceptable. As David Bridges (1986, p. 21) has noted, although controversies occur in all areas of human thought,

> in general, it is not the teaching of historical, scientific or even aesthetic controversy which is the focus of wider public and political concern and debate, but moral, social and political controversy – issues to do with racism, sexism, peace and nuclear disarmament, unemployment, strikes, Northern Ireland, law and order, poverty, sexual ethics, the political economy...
>
> Controversy may arise because: people are attached to different values; people attach different priority to the same values (compare, for example, socialist and liberal priorities in relation to the values of freedom and justice); people give different interpretations to the same value (e.g., 'peace' can be seen on the one hand as the absence of conflict, and on the other as the absence of oppression, 'equality' can mean treating all the same or treating people according to relevant differences).

The ILEA Inspectorate has made a similar observation in its report, *The Teaching of Controversial Issues in Schools*:

> A controversial issue is a matter which different individuals and groups interpret and understand in differing ways and about which there are conflicting courses of action. It is an issue for which society has not found a solution that can be universally accepted. It is an issue of sufficient significance that each of the proposed ways of dealing with it is objectionable to some sections of the community and arouses dissent, opposition or protest. When a course of action is formulated that virtually all sectors of society accept, the issue is no longer controversial. There is much more to a controversial issue than the content of what is studied. The ways in which pupils study a subject, which in itself may have general approval, can also create discord.
>
> (ILEA, 1986, p. 5)

A form of subversion?

In view of this inevitable clash of values, it is not surprising that responses to political education tend to be emotive and the debate between its advocates and detractors, highly charged. As we have indicated elsewhere (Carrington and Short, 1987), there is a popular misconception, especially prevalent on the Right, that teachers committed to political education are a potentially subversive force, seeking to foment unrest among young people by actively propagating anti-establishment and even anti-democratic attitudes and beliefs in the classroom. Drawing attention to this allegation in her Dimbleby lecture, Mary Warnock (1985) observed that 'teachers are sometimes regarded as dangerous' and that 'parents may fear that their children are being indoctrinated with certain social and political beliefs which they, the parents, do not share' (p. 10). She contends that this fear has 'done immense harm to the relations between parents and teachers'. However widespread this fear may be, it is without any real empirical foundation, as Tony Jeffs' recent appraisal of the literature on contemporary curricular practice has indicated. He notes:

> Scant evidence exists of overt political indoctrination by teachers. Gaspar reports that he encountered nothing that could be termed as 'gross bias' (1985), a view endorsed by an HMI who found that 'the vast majority of teachers who are attempting to teach controversial issues... are desperately trying hard to do it with a degree of professional integrity' (Slater, 1984: 8). Perhaps not surprisingly Reid unearthed little community concern over the teaching of politics and in all the schools visited 'an absence of parental antipathy' (1985: 7). Available evidence certainly indicates that Clause 45 of the 1986 Education Act which makes it mandatory 'where political issues are brought to the attention of pupils... they are offered a balanced presentation of opposing views' is unwarranted and gratuitous. Worse, rather than guaranteeing open and balanced debate, it may simply stifle creative discussion in the classroom. For if the legal responsibility to ensure 'balance' obliges teachers to include in their pesentation the views and material of such groups as the NF (National Front), which could not but be offensive to certain pupils, then from the

highest motives many teachers will eschew discussion of certain 'controversial' issues.

(Jeffs, 1988)

The situation described by Jeffs could be exacerbated further by the Educational Reform Act (1988), if Robin Richardson's pessimistic assessment proves to be correct. According to Richardson (1988, p.21), the legislation will ensure 'that, so far as possible, teachers avoid teaching about controversial subjects. Most of the time, the new National Curriculum will prevent controversy arising'.

The commitment to counter authoritarianism, which has become a central concern of initiatives to develop political literacy (see Harber, 1984), provides further evidence to refute charges of anti-democratic intent. Those who subscribe to this particular view of political education generally attach high priority to political autonomy as an educational aim and thus see the school as having a legitimate role in providing young people with a knowledge of political issues, so that they may eventually be in a position to make rational political judgements and thus be 'able to decide which form of political organization is the one to support' (Phillips, 1983, p. 17). Unequivocal in their commitment to the principle of participatory democracy, the proponents of this approach to political education stress that a diversity of attitudes, values and practices should be recognized in the classroom, and that pupils ought to be encouraged to become informed sceptics, empathetic towards those holding different views from their own. Notwithstanding this, the approach in question is *not* predicated upon an acceptance of the untenable relativism encapsulated in the slogan 'Anything Goes', for its advocates insist that it is incumbent upon teachers to maintain and uphold the 'open society' (see Wringe, 1984).

Much of the criticism of political education as currently conceived and practised would, therefore, appear to be ill-informed. Certainly, the model of political education described here, with its emphasis on open discussion and free access to information, may be regarded as antipathetical to the notion of indoctrination: that is, 'the intentional inculcation of values and beliefs as truths' (Harber, 1984, p. 117). Yet despite this, the *fear* of political indoctrination persists, especially at primary level. The 1986 Education Act may be regarded as a direct response to such anxieties. As well as stressing the need for schools to provide pupils with 'a balanced presentation of opposing views', it also proscribes 'the pursuit of partisan political activities by any of those registered pupils at the school who are junior pupils' (DES, 1986, para. 44).

The case for teaching controversial issues in the primary school

Having examined some of the constraints which currently militate against the teaching of politically contentious issues, we will now consider the case for political education in the primary school. In view of the apparent tendency for teachers in this sector to underestimate the extent of children's political awareness and knowledge and their ability to handle certain types of cognitive task, we begin with an appraisal of the relevant psychological literature.

Until comparatively recently, psychologists have tended to stress the intellectual limitations of young children and, in the main, have largely endorsed Piaget's influential theory of cognitive development. In his view, cognitive development can be characterized in terms of a series of discrete 'stages', each having its own distinctive cognitive style and structure. Among other things, his work suggests that children under the age of seven or thereabouts are generally incapable of logical thought, because they tend to be taken in by appearances and interpret experience in an entirely egocentric manner. Between the ages of about seven and 11, the average child develops an ability to reverse actions mentally, though only in so far as they refer to 'concrete' situations. At this 'stage', most children can also focus their thinking on several aspects of a problem at any given time, and are thus in a position where they can relate ideas to one another. According to Piaget (e.g., 1926), however, children do not normally develop the capacity for abstraction and logico-deductive reasoning (formal operations) until after the age of 11. This theory was subsequently extended by Piaget to cover the development of moral thinking, an area especially germane to the teaching of controversial issues (Piaget, 1932). He held that children below six or seven usually subscribe to a way of thinking in which rules are looked upon as 'God-given' (i.e., fixed and immutable) and punishment regarded as the inevitable outcome of their transgression. Also, at this 'stage', ethical judgements are generally based on consequences rather than intentions. (For example, Piaget (1932, p. 118) described the following situation to the children in his study: there are two boys, one of whom, when called to dinner, accidentally breaks 15 cups; the other boy, taking advantage of his mother's absence, accidentally breaks a single cup, while helping himself to jam. When Piaget then asked which of the two is the naughtier, he found that children aged seven and below were more likely to say the first boy; his older respondents thought otherwise.) Children of junior school age, in contrast, tend to employ an autonomous morality where rules are seen as arbitrary, the acceptance of immanent justice is less evident and intention assumes a more prominent role in moral judgement.

During the five decades or so which have elapsed since the initial dissemination of Piaget's findings, many psychologists and educationalists have drawn upon his theory to investigate various aspects of development. These include the growth of interpersonal and moral understanding and children's changing conceptions of social class, gender, authority, government and national identity. (For a comprehensive review of this research, see Leahy, 1983.) The research in question generally corroborates Piaget's views about young children's lack of cognitive sophistication (in particular, their apparent inability to think in abstract terms) and provides a prima facie case *against* the teaching of controversial issues in the primary school. This is not to say, however, that they, or Piaget's original work, should be accepted at face value. Following the publication of seminal studies by Bryant (1974), Gelman (1978) and Hughes (1975), among others, psychologists have increasingly come to accept that Piaget and his followers grossly underestimated children's cognitive ability in a number of areas. The work of Olive Stevens (1982) on the development of children's political consciousness and understanding is a case in point. Working with a sample of 800 children aged between seven and 11 she found that concepts of democracy, leadership and political accountability were accessible to nine-year-olds; some children within this age group were also able to consider alternative social and political arrangements and to justify them in terms of principles. Since this ability is normally associated in Piagetian theory with the 'stage' of formal operations, she asks whether the boundaries between this so-called 'stage' and others is as hard and fast as previously thought. She noted that children of seven 'found no difficulty in joining in political discussion' and had 'some cognitive contact with the political world [encompassing] political information, awareness and, not least, interest' (Stevens, 1982, pp. 32–8). Eleven-year-olds were found to be able to link 'politics not only with roles, structures and policies, but with topics such as conservation, women's rights and an economic reorganization of the country' (p. 150). In contrast to much previous research, Stevens' work not only serves to debunk some of the myths relating to children's alleged political naivety, but also reinforces the view that political education can begin at junior school.

Other research has suggested that a case can be made for dealing with fundamental issues relating to social justice, equality and power in the primary curriculum. The literature on children's understanding of gender and racial differences is especially important in this respect. For instance, as the work of Phyllis Katz (1983) in the United States has shown, both gender and racial identities are established during the pre-school years: children below the age of three are generally able to differentiate on the basis of gender, although 'the foundations of racial awareness and concepts probably develop somewhat later'. (The available evidence on the development of racial awareness is critically appraised in the following chapter.)

The research of Deanna Kuhn and her colleagues (1978) with two- and three-year-olds, not only revealed a high level of agreement with adult stereotypes, but showed that the children thought positively about their own sex and negatively about the other. To elicit her data, Kuhn read the children various statements including 'I'm strong' and 'When I grow up I'll fly an airplane', and then asked them to say which of two dolls ('Lisa' or 'Michael') would be most likely to have made the statement. Although there would appear little question that by the age of five many children have internalized prevailing gender stereotypes about 'appropriate' occupations for women and men and 'appropriate' toys for girls and boys (Katz, 1983), the ascription by gender of stereotypical personality traits (e.g., passivity, aggression, assertiveness, competitiveness) does not occur until somewhat later. To illustrate this development progression, David Best and his associates (1977) presented a large sample of five-, eight- and 11-year-olds (drawn from the United States, Eire and Britain) with a male and female silhouette. The children were provided with descriptive statements (embodying a range of gender stereotypes) and asked to indicate which of the silhouttes best fitted the description. They found that although the bulk of their five-year-olds *did not* consistently employ such stereotypes, three-quarters of the eight-year-olds and virtually all of the 11-year-olds did. The traits that children found easiest to differentiate by gender were those having a relatively familiar concrete referent (e.g., aggression).

These findings have been broadly corroborated in many other studies. William Damon (1977), for example, focusing on gender stereotyping among children aged between four and nine, read his respondents a story about a little boy called George who (despite his parents' disapproval) wished to play with dolls. The children were asked a number of questions, including: 'Why do people tell George not to play with dolls?'; 'Are they right?'; and 'Is there a rule that boys should not play with dolls?'. Although the four-year-olds in the study thought it quite legitimate for George to play in this way, the six-year-olds said that it was wrong (believing that what boys *generally* do and what they *ought* to do are synonymous). In contrast, the older children in the sample were able to see that gender roles were socially and culturally conditioned. As one nine-year-old remarked, 'Breaking windows you're not supposed to do. And if you [boys] play with dolls, well you can, but boys usually don't' (Damon, 1977, p. 263).

Although there is never a simple and unilinear relationship between attitudes and behaviour, research on gender differences in classroom interaction in infant and junior schools has shown *inter alia* that male pupils: generally dominate classroom talk; monopolise school resources (including the playground); and, often because of their boisterousness, receive more of the teachers' time and attention (e.g., Clarricoates, 1980; French and French, 1986).

The case for teaching about controversial issues (such as sexism and racism) in the primary school is further strengthened by research on bias in children's reading materials. During the past decade or so numerous commentators have criticized the values, beliefs and assumptions which continue to underpin many popular picture-books, reading schemes, children's fiction, school texts, comics and magazines (e.g., Zimet, 1976; Tucker, 1981; Stones, 1983; Rice, 1987). Certainly when the content of such materials is considered, the evidence of political consciousness among seven- to 11-year-olds, and sexism and racism among even younger children, becomes all the more convincing. While we recognize the importance of other influences on children's socialization (e.g., the family, television, peer group), we would argue, nevertheless, that reading materials play a vital role in the formation of a person's world-view and her or his perceptions of themselves and others. If primary teachers are to make meaningful interventions to foster the development of their pupils' political and moral understanding, it will be incumbent upon them both to take account of ideological bias when selecting reading materials, and to ensure that children are provided with the necessary skills to begin to detect such bias for themselves. As Steve Whitley's (1988) recent overview has shown, although publishers have taken heed of the criticisms levelled against them since the 1970s, 'very few books contain strong, positive main characters which are black' or 'acknowledge the multiracial nature of British society' (except in a tokenistic or stereotypical manner). Citing the work of Rice (1987) and others, he also shows how some of the best-selling reading schemes (e.g., *Ginn 360*, *Link Up* and *Storychest*) continue to reinforce the marginality of black people and stereo-typical views and attitudes towards them. Although he notes 'the picture in the area of gender is rosier than that in the area of race', many reading schemes and texts often fail to challenge prevailing conceptions of masculinity and femininity, or the status quo between the sexes. In addition to this 'all-white', male-dominated world', Whitley indicates that contemporary reading schemes and young children's books not only persist in giving undue emphasis to middle-class lifestyles and values (by depicting 'cosy, comfortably-off households where children are well-supplied with toys'), but often shield their readers from such issues as 'homelessness, poverty and want'.

Unless teaching about fundamental issues relating to social justice and equality begins in the primary school, pupils' attitudes and beliefs may become so entrenched that subsequent attempts to change them will be less likely to succeed (Lane and Lane, 1987; White, 1983). Primary schools, in contrast to other often more arbitrary, parochial and particularistic agencies of socialization (e.g., the media, family and peer group), can provide children with the opportunity to explore such issues in a systematic and structured fashion.

Furthermore, there may be other important reasons why curricu-lar initiatives directed towards the goal of participatory democracy should begin *prior* to the secondary stage. As David Hicks (1987) has

Bryant. 1984 quoted by Carrington & Short 1989.

recently noted, in relation to the extant research on children's attitudes to countries and cultures other than their own, whereas children as young as five are 'beginning to acquire likes and dislikes about other groups of people', those aged between eight and 12 'do seem to be potentially more tolerant and open'.

We would also cite the work of the influential psychologists Lev Vygotsky (1956), Jerome Bruner (1960) and Gordon Allport (1954) in support of the claim that children in the primary school are 'ready' to benefit from teaching about controversial issues. In contrast to Piaget who held that 'teachers play an insignificant role in children's cognitive development' (Bryant, 1984, p. 252), the authors in question present a forceful argument to show that the teacher's role is crucial. Vygotsky, for example, claims that intellectual potential cannot be conceived as some innate physiological property, but rather must be viewed as a quality created in and through the process of education and socialization. He distinguishes between children's existing development' and their 'potential development'. 'Existing development' refers to those cognitive tasks which they can undertake *without* assistance. Vygotsky refers to the gap between these two levels of development as 'the zone of the next development'. The gap, in the words of Andrew Sutton (1983) 'indicates what the child is ready to master next on the basis of present achievements, given the best possible adult attention' (p. 196).

Vygotsky's strictures are congruent with Bruner's (1960) famous dictum that 'any subject can be taught to any child of any age in an honest way'. To qualify this statement, he notes:

> Research on the intellectual development of the child highlights the fact that at each stage of development the child has a characteristic way of viewing the world and explaining it to himself. The task of teaching a subject to a child at any particular age is one of representing the structure of that subject in terms of the child's way of viewing things.
>
> (Bruner, 1960, p. 33)

Much the same point had in fact been made by Allport (1954) six years earlier when describing teaching strategies to combat racism and prejudice. In Allport's view:

> The age at which these lessons should be taught need not worry us. If taught in a simple fashion all the points can be made

intelligible to younger children and, in a more fully developed way, they can be presented to older students... In fact... through 'graded lessons' the same content can, and should, be offered year after year.

(Allport, 1954, p. 511)

Teaching approaches

The case for teaching controversial issues in the primary school rests not only on children's understanding of such issues and their knowledge of political socialization, but also, as we have argued, on the need to educate the young for participatory democracy. Having demonstrated the primary schoolchild's abilities in the sphere of political education, we now consider various pedagogic strategies to promote it. We begin by looking at the 'neutral chair' and some of its implications.

This approach to handling controversial issues was initially developed by Laurence Stenhouse and his colleagues when devising the Humanities Curriculum Project (1970). It requires teachers to ensure that while all viewpoints are represented (either through pupils' verbal contributions or published source material), their own position is kept strictly under wraps, i.e. is never made known to the pupils. Although this particular means of dealing with controversy in schools has attracted various prominent supporters over the years (e.g., Jeffcoate, 1979; Ruddock and Plaskow, 1985), it has also been the subject of much criticism. In respect of teaching about 'race', for example, David Milner (1983) has written:

> It is ironic that in 1965 the government outlawed incitement to racial hatred in public places, while in the 1980s Jeffcoate is still prepared to countenance the childhood equivalent in the classroom. This is not the intention of the teacher's recommended strategy, but it is probably the effect'.
>
> (Milner, 1983, p. 220)

A further criticism has recently been levelled by Basil Singh (1988). He maintains that while procedural neutrality is premissed upon the assumption that teachers can influence the political views of their pupils, there is, in fact, no experimental evidence to support the premise. On the contrary, Stenhouse and Verma's (1981) evaluation of an antiracist initiative with secondary schoolchildren showed that teachers who made explicit their opposition to racism were no more successful in changing attitudes than those committed to the neutral chair. Thus, whatever the benefits of neutrality may be, a diminution in the teacher's powers of persuasion is, apparently, not one of them.

Finally, we consider the objections raised by Robert Stradling and his colleagues (1984). They argue that 'it simply is not possible to lay down hard and fast rules about teaching controversial subject matter to be applied to all times' (p. 11). As we indicate in Chapter 5, when discussing collaborative group work techniques, some teaching and learning styles lend themselves more than others to procedural neutrality. It is an approach more likely to succeed in situations where pupils are willing and able to voice a range of beliefs and opinions and where they are actively encouraged to listen to the views of others, show tolerance and a respect for evidence. It is unlikely to succeed in settings where didacticism prevails which, sadly, as the work of Biott (1987) and Galton (1987) has shown, remains the predominant form of pedagogy in primary schools. Having acknowledged that procedural neutrality, under certain conditions, may provide an appropriate means of dealing with controversial issues in schools, we would like to reinforce the point made earlier in this chapter, and alluded to by Milner (1983), concerning the dangers of teachers espousing a weak relativist ethic in the classroom. There will always be occasions when teachers have to make their partisanship unequivocal. The expression of racist, sexist and other antidemocratic sentiments are cases in point.

Regardless of whether teachers choose to declare or conceal their views on an issue, we believe it imperative that questions of 'race' and racism are dealt with in a holistic manner. As Troyna (1987) has pointed out, ideological phenomena such as racial scapegoating cannot be challenged effectively if pupils are unable to consider alternative and more plausible explanations of unemployment, urban decay and other socioeconomic problems. He insists that:

the issues of 'race' and ethnic relations (must not be) considered in isolation: rather they need to be seen and considered as pertinent aspects of the social structure along with, say, class and gender. This demands a more broadly based approach, the rejection of pre-packaged 'teaching about race relations' materials and the generation of key concepts around which teaching sessions might be based.

(Troyna, 1987, p. 316)

We would also argue that shielding antiracism from the limelight may paradoxically strengthen its appeal, for by sharing the stage with attempts to obviate other forms of inequality, it is less likely to be perceived as an attempt to proselytise. If 'the medium is the message', children who interpret antiracism as a form of preaching may well resent it and react to such teaching with either indifference or outright hostility.

It has recently been suggested that antisemitism can provide a useful point of departure for teaching about 'race' and ethnic relations in a holistic manner. According to Harvey Monte (1986, p. 26):

A study of anti-semitism offers a unique opportunity to examine racism and prejudice because [it] knows no colour-boundaries and [can therefore] be discussed without the particular kinds of tension that exist when the persecuted are present along with the persecutors... It could also prove useful to examine the experience of Jewish immigrants, particularly in the years of this century... Their experience in schools and communities where they lived were very similar to those of black people today... Finally, teaching about anti-semitism is important as an example of what can still happen to an ethnic minority even when it seems to have succeeded economically, socially and politically.

While we fully support Monte's recommendations, we also share his scepticism concerning the prospects for their implementation. Making much the same criticism of the definition of racism as 'prejudice + power' as we made in Chapter 1, he notes that, as a consequence, antiracists fail to take sufficient account of anti-semitism. He argues that it is 'particularly difficult' to formulate a policy on this form of oppression because 'Jews cannot claim that they are under represented in the Establishment, or that they have no position of influence in the business and professional world' (p. 23).

Summary

We have suggested a number of reasons why the teaching of controversial issues should take place in the primary school. We have argued that much of the criticism of such teaching is not only ill-informed but, in relation to children's knowledge and understanding of such issues, is also theoretically suspect and empirically unsound. The evidence we have reviewed suggests that because of their degree of political sophistication and awareness, primary-aged children are unlikely to ignore the range of ideological bias encountered on television, in books, magazines and comics, and in graffiti on the playground wall. Although, as we have indicated, there is a considerable body of research on children's responses to forms of structural inequality (whether of 'race', class or gender), there remain significant gaps in the literature. In the following chapter, we illustrate our concern in the area of 'race' and racism.

3
Children, 'Race' and Research: A Critique

As we have already indicated, primary teachers are sometimes reluctant to accept that younger children can hold incipient racist attitudes and exhibit hostility towards members of other groups. In this chapter, we engage with the popular belief that younger children are 'colour-blind' and free from the malign influences of individual racism. To this end, we appraise the research on children and 'race'. Various studies are reviewed, both from Britain and the United States, including some conducted many years ago. The historical perspective is important, for it is our contention that fundamental weaknesses in the earlier research continue to disfigure and invalidate some contemporary studies in this area. Although we discuss a range of issues relating to research design and methodology, our concerns are not merely rarefied academic ones. We recognize that over the years such research has had an impact upon educational policy formation, curriculum design and, as a consequence, on some teachers' working lives. We are also mindful of the fact that an increasing number of teachers now conduct small-scale research in their own classrooms. Hopefully, some of the issues raised in the chapter will be of direct relevance to them.

Racial attitudes in white children

The origin and development of children's racial ideas have been of interest to researchers ever since the publication of Bruno Lasker's (1929) pioneering study *Race Attitudes in Children*. His data derived from a questionnaire sent to 'correspondents known to be interested in race relations', and from unsolicited letters he received containing illustrative material. In view of the known unreliability of this means of gathering data, it is of interest to note the similarity between some of Lasker's observations and the findings of more recent research. For example, he recognized the early onset of individual racism and believed along with such well known authorities as Kenneth Clark (1955) that children never become 'aware of racial difference without a feeling about the matter'. To corroborate this claim, he reported a number of instances such as the following:

> A coloured high-school girl spoke admiringly to a little girl of five or six years of age. The child evinced fear at the greeting and turned to her mother: 'Oh, mama, the nigger spoke to me!'
> (Lasker, 1929, p. 4)

Another early study of the childhood antecedents of individual racism employed an experimental design that differed radically from Lasker's. Eugene Horowitz (1936) worked directly with a group of white boys who were aged between three and 14 and came from schools in both the north and south of the United States. Three tests were used. First, the Ranks Test required subjects to put photographs of 12 faces (four of white children, eight of black) in order of preference. This was followed by the Show Me test which involved subjects selecting from the photographs those children they would want as companions in various imaginary contexts such as going to a party or belonging to a gang. Finally, the Social Situations test was designed to discover whether the children would reject participation in an activity because of the inclusion of a black person. It entailed 15 posed settings that were photographed twice, once with and once without a black boy. The subject simply had to look at each of the photographs and state whether or not he wished to join in with the activity. According to Horowitz (1936, pp. 117–18), the results of this study showed that:

> the development of prejudice against Negroes begins very, very early in the life of the ordinary child. . . . boys barely over five years of age, demonstrated a preference for whites on the Ranks test, the most sensitive of the three tests to small amounts of prejudice.

Now, while Horowitz may have been correct in his assertion about the early onset of individual racism in white children, the methodological flaws in the study render the data susceptible to alternative interpretations. For example, in the light of critiques of Piaget's work (e.g., Donaldson, 1978) we might begin by asking whether the tasks made 'human sense' to the children. What, for instance, is one supposed to make of a request to decide, *from pictures alone*, whether to invite a black or white individual to a party? (the Show Me test). Admittedly, there may be *some* children for whom 'race' is of such overriding importance in their social relationships that they would indeed draw up a guest list partly along racial lines. For them, the task must have appeared straightforward. But for children who harbour no ill-feeling towards black people, and who are thus likely, when faced with decisions of this kind, to accord priority to factors other than 'race', the task would probably seem bizarre. To make sense of it, they might quite reasonably assume that the experimenter was really testing their knowledge of cultural norms. In other words, Horowitz was asking who they should choose in order to comply with social convention. (The same criticism applies with equal force to the other two tests.) If a significant proportion of the children did, indeed, construe the task demands in this way, the results of the study are as disturbing as they are misleading. For the children may well have inferred that they not only had to respond in accordance with convention, but that the conventional view was the correct one. (Horowitz's failure to provide his subjects with the option of expressing no preference for either the black or the white figure strengthens this suspicion.) Thus, by reinforcing the social stereotype of black people as generally undesirable, Horowitz could have broken new ground in ways that he neither anticipated nor recognized. As we make clear, these unforeseen and damaging consequences may have been reproduced on many subsequent occasions.

A final criticism of Horowitz's study concerns its external validity; that is, the extent to which the results relate to the real world. As already noted, the data may actually be measuring something other than racial prejudice or individual racism and thus not relate at all to the real world in the way that was intended. But whether this is the case or not, the concept of individual racism needs clarification. Horowitz implies that it is unidimensional; in other words, that white children either like or dislike black people and cling to this view regardless of location or situation. Gordon Allport (1954) also appeared to embrace this notion when he described his three-stage model of prejudice acquisition. He referred to the second stage as one of total rejection and claimed that children at this point in their lives (between the ages of approximately seven and ten) (p. 309): 'will undoubtedly reject all Negroes, in all circumstances and with considerable feeling'.

This is a rather sweeping claim to make in view of the evidence that Allport adduces in support. He cites the work of Blake and Dennis (1943) who asked 60 questions (such as 'Which are more musical – Negroes or white people?'and 'Which are more clean?') to an all-white group of children aged between ten and 17. According to Allport (p. 309):

> these children had, by the age of 10, learned to reject the Negro category totally. No favourable quality was ascribed to Negroes more often than to whites. [Furthermore] this totalized rejection certainly starts earlier... [by the age of seven or eight].

The criticisms that we levelled at Horowitz's work concerning the way that children might interpret the task demand, especially in the absence of a 'neither' or 'both' response option, applies equally to Blake and Dennis' study. But perhaps of more importance is the fact that other research has challenged the notion of total rejection. In a study that one of us conducted in south-east England (Short, 1981), white boys and girls aged between seven and ten were presented with line drawings of two boys (one black, the other white) who were engaged in confrontation. Those children who accused the black figure of having started the trouble were subsequently asked why the white 'child' was being punished by a black 'teacher'. Children required to explain this situation 'were either unable to do so, assumed that they had previously given an incorrect answer or blamed the child himself'. As no child was critical of the teacher, it was concluded:

> Allport's hypothesis cannot be sustained. Prejudice within the age range and social class sampled appears to be situation specific in the sense that a child's antipathy towards children of another 'race' does not necessarily generalise to teachers of that 'race'.
> (Short, 1981, p. 203)

Further confirmation that the nature of individual racism is more complex than Horowitz implies comes from another study conducted in England. Nicola Madge (1976) worked with a group of young children aged between six and eight who were drawn from two multiracial schools in London. She set out to examine 'whether attitudes towards skin colour *vary with context*' (original emphasis). Racial preferences were determined in three different ways. The first was in the form of sociometric data where the children were asked individually to name their best friends in school. The second, a photographs test, involved presenting each child with a pair of photographs (of a black and a white figure) and asking, 'Which do you like best?' The Stories test also involved asking whether they liked a black or white child best but the context in this case was a short piece of fiction in which either the black or white child received approval while the other was reprimanded. Madge concluded:

> These data point to the difficulty of generalising from ethnic preferences observed in test situations. As both racial groups showed in-group orientation in some contexts and out-group orientation in others, the apparent preference of white or black skin colour in one situation does not necessarily mean the rejection of the other. An attempt to quantify children's preferences would thus appear to be misdirected. The nature of the situation . . . and the other variables available on which choices can be based, will influence the extent and direction of racial orientation.
>
> (Madge, 1976, pp. 343–4)

It is thus difficult to predict precisely how, if at all, the racism identified by Horowitz and others will manifest itself in reality. Not only are children liable to say different things in different contexts, but what they say may bear no relation to the way they behave (LaPiere, 1934). Allport (1954) was clearly aware of this possibility. Commenting on the stage of total rejection he noted:

> Around the age of eight, children often *talk* in a highly prejudiced manner. They have learned their categories and their totalised rejection. But the rejection is chiefly verbal. While they may damn the Jews, the wops, the Catholics, they may still *behave* in a relatively democratic manner.
>
> (Allport, 1954, p. 310)

An alternative approach to investigating children's racial attitudes has been to focus quite explicity upon their knowledge of cultural stereotypes. The approach was originally adopted in the United States by Blake and Dennis (1943) and by Radke *et al.* (1950) but it has also been employed in this country. Geoffrey Brown and Susan Johnson (1971), for example, asked white children aged between three and 11 to ascribe positive and negative behavioural characteristics to illustrations of white and 'shaded' figures. Eight 'stories' were read to individual children who then had to point to the 'black' or white figure they thought was being described on each occasion. The stories included the following:

One of the boys has broken a window with a stone. Which boy do you think threw the stone?

One of the boys is very good and goes to the shop for his mummy. Which do you think is the good boy?

One of the girls is a bully and hits the other one. Which do you think is the bad girl?

One of the girls works very hard at school and the teacher likes her. Which do you think works hard?

Now the criticisms we have made of Horowitz's research, and that of Blake and Dennis would seem to apply *a fortiori* to this study by Brown and Johnson. Once again the task is confusing, if not fatuous, as the children have no rational basis upon which to reach a decision. For how can one possibly tell, just by looking at a photograph, whether a boy 'goes to the shop for his mummy' or if a girl 'works very hard at school'? Clearly, the children were left with the option of making a guess (that *could have been* influenced by their attitude) or relying on their knowledge of racial stereotypes. Either way, it is difficult to view the data as an accurate guide to the children's racial attitudes.

Among their observations, Brown and Johnson found that ten-year-olds showed 'a small but significant decrease in prejudice'. They offer no explanation but note that both Horowitz and Horowitz (1938) and Radke *et al.* (1950) 'commented upon a similar decrease in prejudice scores around 10 years of age'. One possible explanation for this finding is that by the age of ten, children have become aware of the dangers that may arise from answering questions 'correctly'. In relation to studies of racism, of course, the danger lies in being labelled a racist, and it may be that ten-year-olds would rather avoid this accusation than demonstrate their know-ledge of racial stereotypes. Alternatively, it may be the case that at around ten years of age, children recognize tasks of this kind as having no discernible logic and are therefore inclined to act in a random and *apparently* less prejudiced manner.

Of more concern than the correct interpretation of Brown and Johnson's data is the likely impact of the research act itself, on the children's thinking about 'race'. For the sort of questions that were asked not only test the child's awareness of stereotypes but, arguably, as in Horowitz's study, reinforce them. If white children already 'know' that members of the black community are personae non gratae because of what they hear from parents and peers, see on television and read in books and comics, then to be asked such questions as, 'Which do you think is the good boy?', will, in all probability, serve only to strengthen and entrench existing preju-dicies. Of course, for some of Brown and Johnson's subjects, the whole area of racial and ethnic stereotyping may have been virgin territory. In such cases, the research act functions as an introduction to individual racism, for by insisting that they select either the black or the white figure, rather than both or neither, they are led to believe that one racial group is morally, and in other ways, superior to another. (For a further discussion of this issue in relation to research on teachers' attitudes, see Troyna and Carrington, 1988.)

Recent research

The weaknesses and damaging implications of much of the research we have reviewed so far have surfaced more recently in studies by Alf Davey and his colleagues (Davey, 1983) and by Braha and Rutter (1980).

The children with whom Davey worked were of white, West Indian and Asian origin, aged between seven and ten and drawn from schools in London and Yorkshire. They were given various tests, one of which dealt with stereotypes. The task entailed presenting children with statements such as, 'These are clever people' and 'These people make trouble' and then asking them to 'post' the statements into one of four boxes. Three of the latter were identified by photographs of adult couples representing either 'Whites', 'West Indians' or 'Asians', and the fourth was labelled 'Nobody'. Now in so far as this test allowed the children an opportunity not to stereotype, it was clearly an advance on much previous research. Nevertheless, for those children who already 'knew' or at least suspected that West Indians 'make trouble', the test could be perceived as validating their 'knowledge', and to this extent it remains vulnerable to the charge of reinforcing stereotypes. (In view of this speculation, it is of interest to note that Davey (1983, p. 162) actually refers to an interview with a white parent who said of her son: 'He asks me why there are so many blacks here that they make trouble.') An equally serious problem concerns the way in which the statements were worded, for any remark that begins 'These people...' encourages children to think about individuals in terms of their group membership rather than their personal qualities, and such thinking arguably constitutes the basic building blocks of racial prejudice and racialist behaviour.

Other task demands employed by Davey, while perhaps not actually damaging the children, must surely have confused them. In the Paired Comparisons test, for example, the children were shown a pack of 12 photographs representing both sexes of the three ethnic groups, well-dressed and poorly dressed. On the presentation of each pair, the child was to say which one was liked best! Precisely what this test is supposed to be measuring in terms of its real world implications is difficult to assess, but according to Davey (p. 118), the results show that, 'as far as the white children are concerned, a poorly dressed white child is preferable to any member of another group no matter how they are dressed'. Now, if this is true, it can only be so within the severely restricted and artificial conditions of the psychologist's laboratory. Beyond such narrow confines the conclusion has to be less plausible, for it neglects the influence of context.

Another of Davey's tasks, the Limited Choice test, required each child 'to share sweets between (representatives of different racial groups) photographed in the park'. For children holding overtly racist views, this task would presumably pose few difficulties. Other things being equal, they would have no compunction or hesitation in discriminating against pictures of black people. But for children with less well-honed attitudes to 'race', the task might be difficult to take seriously, for most people in the real world take other factors than 'race' into account when distributing largesse.

Potentially, the most interesting aspects of Davey's work were not explored at all. These were the reasons that the children had for responding as they did. In relation to the Limited Choice test, for example, it would have been interesting to have asked the 'ethnocentric' children to explain why they chose to give sweets only to members of their own racial group. Similarly, when Davey showed his subjects photographs of 'White', 'West Indian' and 'Asian' children and asked: 'if you could choose, which one would you most like to be?' he failed to probe their reasoning. (It should be noted, incidentally, that with regard to this question, the children were not given an opportunity to express their possible indifference, and as a result, the pro-white bias may have been artificially inflated.) The absence of such elaboration in Davey's work is not atypical of the genre and the value of the entire body of research is much diminished in consequence.

Braha and Rutter (1980), working in a mixed 'race' primary school, set out to explore the relationship between friendship and racial attitude. They tested the latter with the Preschool Racial Attitude Measure 11 (PRAM 11) (Williams *et al.*, 1975) which they describe as follows:

> [PRAM 11] consists of two parallel sets of items, each containing 12 racial-attitude items... For each racial item, the child is shown a picture which includes a pinkish-tan figure and a light brown figure and he is read a short story which asks him to evaluate the two figures. For example... 'There are two little boys. One of them is a kind little boy. Once he saw a kitten fall into a lake and he picked up the kitten to save it from drowning. Which is the kind little boy? The subject scores... 0 when he associates negative characteristics with the white figure (and scores 1 for the opposite response) ... The higher the total score, the more pro-white/anti non-white the child.

Although Braha and Rutter seem oblivious of the contribution they may unwittingly have made to the perpetuation of negative racial stereotypes, they nevertheless recognize the shortcomings of their test as a measure of racial attitudes:

> the materials are such that some children, especially in the older groups, seemed to the experimenter to guess the purpose of the

test and to respond in what they took to be the socially desirable way, namely pro-white.

(p. 221)

As evidence of the unreliability of the test, Braha and Rutter cite the absence of a correlation in their study between racial attitude and friendship choice. In other words, white children with apparently negative attitudes towards black people were no more inclined to choose own-'race' friends than were their white counterparts who, seemingly, were less prejudiced. We share Braha and Rutter's scepticism concerning the value of PRAM 11 but believe they attach undue importance to the correlation between racial attitude and friendship. Only 20 per cent of the school's intake was white. Had the proportion been substantially higher, a rather different pattern of friendship choice might have emerged. This possibility is suggested by a study carried out 30 years earlier by Radke, Sutherland and Rosenberg (1950). They measured the racial attitudes of a group of children (aged seven to 13) in a predominantly black school. The children were asked to attribute a variety of traits such as meanness, aggression and dishonesty to photographs of either a black or white figure. They noted that white children:

> show clearly their acceptance of the attitudes of their culture toward the Negro... in each grade the white children assign many more undesirable than desirable characteristics to Negro photographs.
> (Radke, Sutherland and Rosenberg, 1950, pp. 158 and 160)

The children were then asked to nominate their preferred 'choice of friends' from the same photographs and it was found that the vast majority of white children opted for the white figure. When they were later questioned about their real-life friendships in the class, the school and the community at large, it was again found that white children preferred white friends. In fact, where there were more white children to choose from, as there would be in the community rather than the school, and in the school rather than the class, so the number of white choices increased.

In describing this study, David Milner (1983, p. 114) maintained that 'there is consistency between rejection of the black figures in the picture tests and the children's real life friendship choices'. We cannot dispute this correlation nor would we wish to deny that Braha and Rutter may have obtained similar results had they extended their inquiry beyond the confines of the school. We would, however, take issue with Milner's claim that Radke et al.'s picture tests are a valid measure of 'the form that racial attitudes take during [the years seven to 13]'. Indeed, we believe that these tests are no more valid a measure of racial attitudes than is the PRAM 11. For although they may, under certain circumstances, correlate with friendship choice, it has yet to be established that own–group preference in respect of friendship implies rejection, or any degree of hostility towards an out-group.

The nature of racial preference

As long ago as 1962, Kenneth Morland was at pains to point out that preference is not synonymous with prejudice in so far as the latter implies an overt antipathy towards others. Morland's own study was of nursery children in the southern United States. He found that while 73 per cent of white children expressed an own-'race' preference for playmates, 80 per cent of them were willing to accept non-whites while only 4 per cent displayed an active rejection. Similarly, McCandless and Hoyt (1961), working in the United States, with three- to five-year-old Asian-American and white children noted evidence of cleavage but not of avoidance by one group of the other.

Further support for the view that preference does not necessarily imply rejection, arises from an analysis of different approaches to sociometry. The most popular of these aproaches, known as peer nomination, requires children to choose a limited number of friends with whom they wish to associate in various situations. For instance, Moreno (1934), who pioneered the technique, asked children to select two classmates whom they wished to sit between. He discovered (p. 61) 'From about the fifth grade... the beginnings of a racial cleavage' by which he meant a tendency on the part of one group of children to select own-'race' friends. However, some later investigations conducted in Britain, suggest that racial cleavage often begins at a much younger age. Rowley (1968), for example, working with seven- to 15-year-olds found the youngest most likely to choose same 'race' friends, and Duorojaiye's (1969) study of junior age children, showed that in-group preferences were highest among the eight-year-olds.

Although these studies of racial preference may be of theoretical interest and also have practical application, it is important to realize that for a number of reasons, they cannot be seen as evidence of out-group rejection. To begin with, as Davey (1987a) points out, the Criswell Index used to measure in-group bias, is 'a summarising statistic which can conceal individual differences'. Thus the overall tendency for children to prefer own-group friends says nothing about the number of such children who have no wish for ethnic exclusivity. On a related note, Ken Thomas (1984, p. 66) argues:

> there is one major, often unacknowledged, potential source of bias in the peer-nomination technique when applied in this manner. In most studies each child is asked to nominate a limited number of companions according to specified criteria. Yet it is possible that children generally accept their cross-'race' peers without choosing them in any of these categories. As a consequence, an unduly negative picture of children's cross-'race' relationships could be presented in studies where choice restrictions have been imposed.

An alternative sociometric technique designed to overcome this problem is known as Roster-and-Rating. It involves asking each child in a class to rate every other member of the class (usually on a five-point scale) in terms of various criteria. Studies making use of this approach (e.g., Singleton and Asher, 1977), rather than peer nomination, have generally reported a more favourable picture of relations between black and white children. While Roster-and-Rating studies show the continuing influence of 'race' upon children's friendship formation, they emphasize, at the same time, that preference, for one racial group, should not necessarily be construed as rejection of another.

A further reason for exercising caution before equating preference with rejection is that preference itself has been found to vary across situations (cf. Madge, 1976). Davey's (1987a) work, provides us with a recent example. He asked pupils from schools with a substantial white and ethnic minority population to name two children who they would most like to sit next to in class, mix with in the playground and invite home from school. The major finding was that:

> a significant degree of in-group preference characterised the friendship patterns of all three ethnic groups. Furthermore, all three groups were more reluctant to take home friends from a different ethnic background than they were either to sit with them in class or play with them in the playground.
>
> (Davey, 1987a, p. 83)

With this degree of variation, it is clearly misleading to refer to children's racial preferences without specifying the context. Moreover, this particular study suggests that the process of measuring racial preference may be more complex than it seems, for the marked reluctance to take home friends from a different ethnic group may well reflect, to some degree, the influence of parental attitudes. Indeed, we can never be sure when children express a preference in relation to *any* hypothetical social situation, that their preference is unaffected by the opinions of others.

'Hello Dolly!'

In discussing the development of racial attitudes, we have so far concentrated exclusively on those of white children towards the black community. Yet much of the early and subsequent literature has been concerned with the racial attitudes of black children. This area of research began in the United States in the late 1930s with studies of self-identification by nursery school children. Ruth Horowitz (1939) presented photographs of black and white children to her sample of two- to five-year-olds and asked them to point to the one that they most closely resembled. It was found that nearly one-third of the children misidentified. A very similar piece of research was undertaken by Kenneth and Mamie Clark (1939) who requested their three- to five-year-olds to 'Show me which one is you. Which one is [name of subject]?' The proportion of black children in this study who saw themselves as white was more than 40 per cent although some of the older children seem to have had difficulty in understanding what was required of them (p. 597): '[they] refused to identify themselves with any picture saying "I'm not on there" or "that's not me" or "I don't know them" etc.'

Undoubtedly, the best known of these early studies of black children's racial attitudes was carried out by the same authors (Clark and Clark, 1947). Their sample comprised 253 three- to seven-year-olds who came from schools in both the north and south of the United States. Their skin colour was described as either 'dark brown to black', 'light brown to dark brown' or 'practically white'. The children had to select either a black or a white doll in response to questions concerning their preferences (e.g., 'Give me the doll that is a nice doll'), their knowledge of racial differences (e.g., 'Give me the doll that looks like a white child') and their self-identity ('Give me the doll that looks like you').

One of the most publicized findings from this study concerns the children's identification with the white doll. Before commenting further on its significance, though, we wish to draw attention to the context in which the data were gathered. Clark and Clark write:

> Some of the children who were free and relaxed in the beginning of the experiment broke down and cried...during the latter part when they were required to make self-identifications. Indeed, two children ran out of the testing room, unconsolable, convulsed in tears.
>
> (Clark and Clark, 1947, p. 611)

Now while the absence of a precedent may partially exonerate the Clarks from responsibility for this state of affairs, repeating the study under similar circumstances would be difficult to justify. It is clearly reprehensible to ignore ethical issues in the interests of replication, and where the two are in conflict, an alternative and more acceptable methodology must be devised. The past 40 years have not only been barren of such alternatives but, as we point out below, numerous studies have continued to make use of the 1947 format.

It is hard to think of any study in the history of social psychology that has had as much impact on social policy as that achieved by Clark and Clark. For it was their work that provided the Supreme Court with a basis for banning school segregation in 1954. They claimed that roughly one-third of their children chose the white doll in response to the question: 'Give me the doll that looks like you' and that:

approximately two thirds of the subjects indicated... that they like the white doll 'best' or that they would like to play with the white doll in preference to the coloured doll and that the white doll is a 'nice doll'.

(Clark and Clark, 1947, p. 608)

In the 20 years or so following publication of this research, there have been numerous replications, in different parts of the world, which have produced similar findings (see Milner, 1983, or Davey, 1983, for detailed accounts). During the last 20 years, in contrast, levels of mis-identification by black children have dramatically fallen (e.g., Hraba and Grant, 1970; Fox and Jordan, 1973) and this reversal in the trend has generally been attributed to the Black Consciousness movement. However, the degree of out-group identification in the early studies may have been exaggerated. For example, we note that nearly 50 per cent of those children in the Clarks' study who chose the white doll as looking most like them were themselves light skinned and described by the Clarks as 'practically white'. It is thus not surprising that when Greenwald and Oppenheim (1968) included a so-called 'mulatto doll' in their modification of the Clarks' study, there was substantially less out-group identification.

Some commentators have attempted to play down the importance of this experiment either by pointing to its methodological weaknesses or by reinterpreting the data. Milner (1983) falls into the latter category. He bases his criticism partly on the fact that a majority of black children in the study, whether of light, medium or dark skin, indicated the dark doll as looking 'most like a Negro'. He concluded that:

> although the sheer number of children identifying with the white doll was less than in other studies, the proportion of children *not* identifying with the figure who they had maintained was most like their group, was very much the same.
>
> (Milner, 1983, p.152)

Milner argues that children can be said to misidentify when they know which doll looks most like their group but fail to recognize the same doll as looking most like them. However, while the majority of nursery-aged children interviewed by Greenwald and Oppenheim were aware that people referred to as 'Negroes' have dark skins, we have no way of knowing whether the children who chose the white or 'mulatto' doll as most closely resembling themselves, would actually have described themselves as Negro. The chances are, they would not. We therefore believe that Greenwald and Oppenheim were correct to suggest that the misidentification revealed by the Clark and Clark design was, to some degree, an artifact. This suspicion is fuelled further by not knowing the extent to which the misidentification resulted from the children's cognitive limitations. For example, in Greenwald and Oppenheim's experiment, a significant number of *white* children identified with the 'mulatto' doll. This suggests that at a particular stage in their development, children may not understand the concept of a representative figure, or at any rate, are unable to envisage and recognize certain representations of themselves.

Traditionally, black children's identification with the white doll was seen not as an artefact but as a rejection of their own racial group. Mary Goodman (1952), for example, commented:

> The relative inaccuracy of Negro identification reflects not simple ignorance of self, but unwillingness or psychological inability to identify with the brown doll because the child wants to look like the white doll.

Although pro-white responses to preference questions were taken as support for this contention, there is no logical connection between own-group rejection and the type of question devised by the Clarks to test for racial preference. To ask a child to 'Give me the doll that is a nice doll' is essentially meaningless if there are no relevant data upon which to base a decision. Once again, then, we have a situation in which children may have tried to make sense of a senseless demand by responding in terms of their cultural knowledge. In other words, they saw the exercise as a test of their knowledge of racial stereotypes rather than of how they felt about being black. If this interpretation is correct, the children's response to the so-called preference questions cannot be seen as a further manifestation of own-group rejection. (Incidentally, as we noted in relation to Horowitz's work (p. 42), it is rather odd that when children are asked to express a racial preference, either directly or indirectly, they are denied an opportunity to abstain, i.e. to make known their neutrality or indifference. Thus, in the Clarks' study, as in others, the use of a restricted forced choice procedure may have artificially elevated the pro-white response rate.)

Finally, we consider whether autobiographical evidence allows us to equate pre-1970 misidentification with own-'race' rejection. Davey (1987b, p. 478), believing that it does, insists that there were 'times when black people were so oppressed by militant white supremacy that their children wished to be other than they were'. He illustrates this assertion by citing the testimony of well-known black writers and activists. Malcolm X (Haley, 1968), for instance, recalled the pain of:

> 'literally burning my flesh with lye, in order to cook my natural hair until it was limp, to have it look like a white man's hair' (quoted in Milner, 1983, p. 147.)

Whatever the limitations of adult recollection, few would doubt the authenticity of such vivid testimony. But we do not know how many contemporaries of Malcolm X shared his experiences and should not, therefore, assume that his memories reflect a *widespread* own-'race' rejection by black children at that time.

Fortunately, the question of black children's sense of self is no longer a matter of concern, as evidence (e.g., Stone, 1981) suggests that the self concept of both black and white children is now much the same. None the less, many of the methodological and ethical issues thrown up by studies we have reviewed should be kept constantly in mind by those continuing to research in the area of children and 'race'.

Implications for teaching

If we turn now to consider this body of literature from the standpoint of the practising primary teacher, we find that, partly for methodological reasons, its classroom implications are rather vague. The fact that white children, for example, prefer representations of white figures may well have curricular implications for both 'all white' and multiracial schools, but until we know the reasons for their preference, the implications will remain ill-defined. Again, the fact that black children at one time tended to misidentify themselves as white, but no longer do so, is undoubtedly of theoretical and historical interest, but its relevance to the contemporary classroom is difficult to discern.

It is, perhaps, ironic, that the one respect in which existing literature does have clear-cut implications for the teacher results from an unintended by-product of the main experimental design. Specifically, a number of children in different studies, when asked to choose between a black and a white figure, made explicitly racist remarks. Horowitz (1936), for example, refers to 'some incidental comments by test subjects, unsystematically recorded'. These included a three-year-old saying 'I don't like black boys', and a similar remark from a four-year-old. In a well-known British study which investigated the racial attitudes of children in three London boroughs, Isidore Pushkin (1967) asked children to select from a number of dolls (black, white, male and female) those they wished to invite to a birthday party. When a white six-year-old was questioned about why he never chose a black doll, he replied: 'If I have to sit next to one of those, I'll have a nervous breakdown.'

Further evidence for the early onset of racism derives from a more recent British study that marks a radical departure from the traditional doll choice methodology. Robert Jeffcoate (1977) worked in a Bradford nursery school where he asked the teacher to show her children pictures of black people portrayed in a 'variety of situations and in a respectful and unstereotyped way'. When discussing their reactions in front of the teacher, the children's comments could in no way be construed as racially offensive. However, when the same set of pictures were left 'casually' around the room (but in locations close to concealed tape recorders), the remarks made by an equivalent group of children, in the assumed absence of an adult audience, were undeniably racist in tone.

These observations cannot be challenged and dismissed on grounds of their artificiality; nor can they be said to result from unintelligible task demands. They clearly dispel all notions of childhood innocence, as far as 'race' is concerned. Research priorities have to change. We do not need more evidence of racism in young children but rather guidance on how to combat it. In the first instance this means gaining more insight into how children under-stand 'race', the beliefs they have about racial and ethnic differences and how these differences are explained. For no teaching can be effective unless it makes contact with children's existing knowledge.

As well as advocating a shift in research focus, we urge that greater consideration be given to methodological issues. We are not only concerned to avoid the unwitting reinforcement of stereotypes, the construction of ambiguous or fatuous task demands and the unnecessary infliction of pain; we wish also to obviate the constraints implicit within quantitative approaches to research. We believe that the latter, in the interests of statistical analysis constitute a methodological straitjacket in which respondents are inhibited from exploring and revealing the full extent of their understanding of 'race'. Quantitative researchers appear to seek a brief and simple response to an agenda that *they* regard as relevant and important. In effect, children are forced to construe the world in ways that may be quite alien to them and conversely, are denied an opportunity to advance their own ideas on 'race' and 'race'-related matters.

We have attempted to accommodate these criticisms in two research projects. The first, which we report in the following chapter, involved talking to children between the age of six and 12 about various forms of structural inequality. The second, a case study of antiracist teaching with children aged ten to 13, is described in Chapter 5.

4
Talking about Inequality

In concluding our review of the literature on children and 'race', we urged that future research focus rather more on the cognitive than the affective component of racial attitude formation. We suggested, in effect, that the priority traditionally given to researching children's racial feelings be replaced by a greater concern with discovering their knowledge and understanding of racial issues. For as Robin Campbell and Denis Lawton (1970, p. 901) have pointed out, 'if we do not know the nature of children's thinking about society, it is difficult to plan appropriate learning contexts for them'. In this chapter, we report the findings of an exploratory study which attempts to go some way towards meeting Campbell and Lawton's imperative with respect to antiracist teaching. However, we have already argued that such initiatives ought not to be restricted to the issue of 'race' alone, but should address concomitantly a range of structural inequalities. Our investigation, therefore, includes an analysis of the way in which children construe differentiation based on social class and gender in addition to 'race'.

Background to the study

The field work for the study was carried out between February and October 1987. Of the 161 children involved, 56 were top infants (aged between six and eight), 50 were second-year juniors (aged eight to ten) and 55 fourth-year juniors (aged ten to 12). They were drawn from two 'all white' schools in the south of England. Workington Primary was situated in the heart of a housing estate originally built by the local authority. Middleton Primary, in contrast, had a catchment area of relatively large housing built for owner occupation.

Although differences between children from the two schools will be pointed out when appropriate, the study was not designed with this intention. Indeed, any attempt at producing such comparisons would founder on the failure to control for possible differences in ability and other relevant variables such as school ethos. (In this respect, it may be worth noting that while didactic class teaching and a generally 'formal' atmosphere seemed to prevail at Middleton, a somewhat freer and more relaxed approach appeared the norm at Workington – a perception that may have been influenced, to some degree, by the latter's open plan architecture. It should also be noted that, in contrast to Middleton where there was no official policy on 'race', the staff at Workington were in the process of formulating one). The reason for sampling different social backgrounds was simply to provide teachers with some idea of the variety of response to be found among children of this age range to questions of 'race', gender and class.

The actual investigation was undertaken by Geoffrey Short (GS) who initially visited each class on a number of occasions in order to get acquainted with the children. Following these preliminary encounters, each child was invited to select a friend who would accompany them, in the presence of GS, 'to look at and talk about some pictures' in a quiet room. Nobody refused. There were nine pictures altogether, arranged in three sets, one telling a 'story' about 'race', another about gender and the third about social class. A semi-structured interview was conducted and the children's comments tape recorded (with their prior consent). The results of the subsequent content analysis are outlined below.

'Race'

The pictures were displayed in sequence in front of each pair of children. The first showed a black boy leaning against a wall while watching two white children (a girl and a boy) play a ball game. In the second picture the black boy was seen in conversation with the other children and in the third, he was walking away from them, clearly disconsolate. Presenting these pictures to the children served

a threefold purpose; namely, to stimulate interest and encourage participation, to provide an initial basis for testing their awareness of racism and to act more generally as a means of probing their knowledge and understanding of the black experience in contemporary Britain.

The findings

Having seen the pictures, the children were asked to describe what was happening. Without exception, and without prompting, the fourth years assumed that the black boy's rejection could have been racially motivated. The entire second year thought likewise, although in their case, a couple of children in each school only considered 'race' a possible explanation when, in response to their original comment, they were asked to think of any other reason for not allowing the black boy to join in. Although most of the infants also remarked on the racial dimension, *some* would not countenance the idea of discrimination, perhaps, as suggested below, because of a partial or total failure to construe colour as skin pigmentation.

GS: Why don't they want him to play?
Andrew (6:11): He might be a bit rough and naughty.
Matthew (6:11): 'Cos they're mean.
Andrew : 'Cos he won't let them play in his games sometimes.

When asked directly whether the situation could have arisen because of the boy's colour Andrew replied:

No, 'cos I've got lots of friends of different colour. I used to have a friend with red hair. I used to play with her even though she was a different colour.

Although no child thought it fair to prevent the boy from joining in on account of his appearance, the reasons given varied with age. Among the youngest children, only a handful opposed the hypothetical discrimination because it was based on an irrelevance, i.e. the child's racial identity:

Victoria (7:1): It doesn't matter what colour you are, or how tall or how old you are.
Carrie (6:9): [It's not fair] 'cos he's still the same as you but his skin is different...

Most of our six- to eight-year-olds, though, were unable to provide valid grounds for their sense of injustice. They either said what they would do in the circumstances ('If it was my game, I'd let him play'), responded tautologically (claiming the white boy and girl had acted unfairly because 'they are mean and nasty') or simply described the situation without attempting to explain it. In contrast, the accusations of unfairness levelled by the two older groups were invariably well justified. The second years most often argued that 'people are exactly the same except for colour', or that '[the boy] can't help being black'. But a few seemed to ignore or go beyond the salience of 'race', appealing instead to a transcendent ethic:

Adam (9:10): It doesn't matter about their colour. It's how friendly they are. It's what they're like inside that's important.
Simon (8:11): They wouldn't like it if two black people were playing together and one of [the white children] came up and the black people wouldn't let them play.

Adam's dismissal of 'race' as an irrelevance and Simon's paraphrase of the biblical injunction to do as you would be done by, were both mentioned on a couple of occasions by fourth years. However, a clear majority among the latter, in common with the eight- to ten-year-olds, found rejecting the boy on racial grounds objectionable because 'he's just the same [as us] except a different colour'. One of the few differences between the older age groups was the more pronounced tendency of the oldest children to talk explicitly in terms of personality. Neil (11:3), for instance, said that 'black people are just the same underneath as white people; just as cruel as us and just as kind. There's good and bad in both black and white.'

As with many previous studies (e.g., Davey, 1983) we were concerned to discover the children's racial preferences. To provide valid data, however, we considered it necessary to depart from standard practice in several ways. First, we abandoned the demand that respondents opt either for a black or a white identity no matter how ambivalent their attitude. Secondly, we tested for the possibility that they might not wish for the same skin colour as an adult as they would as a child and thirdly, we attempted to find out, rather than to speculate on, the reasons for their preference. The first of two questions on racial preference was therefore as follows: 'If you could choose, as a child, to be black or white, which would you prefer, or are you not bothered?' We found no more than two or three children in our entire sample who expressed a desire to be black and thus, prima facie, the results are consistent with earlier research showing very high levels of in-group preference among white children. (In Davey's case, the proportion was 86 per cent). This finding, though, may be misleading, for the majority within each age group claimed they were not bothered. The picture is complicated further by those second and fourth years who said their decision would depend on the circumstances.

> *Simon* (8:11):   In England I'd prefer to be white 'cos there's more whites; otherwise I wouldn't mind.
> *Ian* (9:4):   I'd rather be the colour what is in the nation. England is normally white; Africa is normally black.
> *Neil* (11:3):   I wouldn't like to be white in somewhere like Brixton.
> *Matthew* (11:1):   If most of my friends were black and I went to a black school, then I wouldn't really mind (what colour I was) but

if I was the only (black) one in a white school, I wouldn't want to be black.

While these comments from the older children might prompt us to question the methodological adequacy of some aspects of extant research, the ideas themselves are quite unambiguous. Unfortunately, the same cannot be said for our infants, many of whom, in response to questions about the nature of 'race', seemed to think about it in ways that make it difficult to interpret their preferences. They were asked why some people are black and others are white, if it is possible to change colour and whether black parents can have a white child and conversely. In reply to all three questions, the infants at Middleton appeared more advanced in their thinking than their counterparts at Workington. A majority of the former, for example, tended to think that people's skin colour depended on their country of origin, while the rest said they were just born like it. At Workington the responses were considerably more varied and certainly more imaginative.

> GS: Why are some people black and others white?
> *Paul* (7:2): It's the things that the ladies eat. They might eat brown sauce and spill it over the baby and the baby might go brown.
> *David* (7:1): Probably their mums were sunbathing and they got brown and the baby came out brown. If mums don't sunbathe, the baby comes out white.
> GS: So, if your mum had been sunbathing, do you think you'd look like (the black boy in the picture)?
> *David*: Yes.

Whereas nearly all the Middleton infants said it was not possible for people to change their skin colour, almost half of those at Workington assumed it was. Among the latter, some like Richard (7:0) thought the issue was rather more complex.

> If you're white and sunbathe too long you can go really brown and look like him [in the picture]. If you're about 18 and are black, you must have been born black 'cos you're too young to change colour, but if you're old (about 50 or 60), and black, you could have been born white and then turned black.

Matthew (6:9), who was also from Workington, claimed that someone born black can become white, 'if they have a bath'.

There was again a marked difference between infants from the two schools over whether parents and their children have to be the same colour. Nearly all of those at Workington thought this was not a necessity; at Middleton, most thought it was.

Not only did many of the six- to eight-year-olds have a rather tenuous grasp on the concept of 'race'; a sizeable proportion also had little awareness of the everyday realities confronting black children. For example, in response to the question, 'What do you think are the worst things about being a black child?' only half of them referred to manifestations of racism suggesting that 'You might get picked on' or 'get called names'. (None thought that teachers would engage in discriminatory behaviour.) The remaining responses ranged from the seemingly innocuous ('You can't see measles or chicken pox'; 'In the dark, other people can't see you'), through to the disparaging ('I don't like the colour black'). In contrast, virtually all the second years saw racism, in some form, as the most serious blight on a black child's life. Most often they remarked on incidents (occasionally including teacher behaviour), that occur within the confines of the school, but one or two, like Claire (9:10), recognized a broader dimension.

> They may chuck all the blacks out of the country and just keep the whites, then the blacks won't have anywhere to live... The government might do that one day.

While the fourth years were also in no doubt about the impact of racism on black children's lives, a few (from Middleton), showed rather more awareness of the subtleties of individual racism. Specifically, they referred to the issue of stereotyping. James (11:4), for instance, thought the worst thing about being black was that 'you'd lose all your friends cos they'd think you're violent'. Stereotyping cropped up again when we asked the infants and second years what advantages, if any, they saw in having a black skin. Although the infants could generally think of none, there were, nevertheless, indications that many of the second years had internalized the popular stereotype of black sporting and athletic prowess (Carrington, 1986).

When we investigated the children's racial preferences as an adult, there was a significant shift among both sets of infants towards neutrality; i.e., they were more inclined to say 'not bothered' than when asked about their childhood preferences. The same was true for the second years from Workington, and to a much lesser extent, of the fourth years from the same school. At Middleton, the second years thought it far more important to have a white skin as an adult than as a child. The oldest children agreed although in their case, the number (in percentage terms) who changed from 'not bothered' to 'white' was much smaller.

We probed the reasoning behind their preferences by asking about the disadvantages of having a black skin as a grown up. Although a substantial minority of our six- and seven-year-olds could not think of any, rather more referred to racial harassment in the form of 'getting picked on' or 'called names'. One or two made comments that illustrate once again just how out of touch infants can be with contemporary black experience. According to Richard (7:0), for instance, the most serious disadvantage facing a black adult is that 'black cats might think you're something like a black animal'. Similarly, Stuart (7:1) said: 'If you're black and a dog came up to you and only liked white people, he would scratch you.'

Racial inequality and discrimination were perceived very differently by a significant number of second years at Middleton. They referred to some of the more pressing socioeconomic constraints encountered by the black community.

> *Simon* (8:11):   They're mostly unemployed.
> *GS*:   Why's that?
> *Simon*:   It's their colour.
> *GS*:   What do you mean?
> *Simon*:   Most [whites] only want their own colour.

Ian (9:4) thought along the same lines.

> *Ian*:   Maybe it would be easier to find a job if you're white.
> *GS*:   Why?
> *Ian*:   'Cos some people in England are racists, so if they have a job to offer, blacks won't get it.
> *GS*:   Is there any other disadvantage in being a black grown-up?
> *Ian*:   Your housing may be restricted in some way.
> *GS*:   What do you mean?
> *Ian*:   Because you're black, if you ask for planning permission over some land, whoever you're asking may not like blacks and say 'we're not going to grant you this piece of land'.

While the second years at Workington restricted their assessment of black disadvantage largely to manifestations of individual racism ('People don't like you'; 'Get called names'), there remained a few who could think of no drawbacks. Among the two groups of fourth years, there was a heightened awareness of discrimination in both employment and (at Middleton) in housing, and one or two children at each school also mentioned problems with the police (cf. Brown, 1986).

The children were then asked if any advantages attached to being a black adult. The overwhelming majority, regardless of age, thought not. Nevertheless, one or two were able to envisage the possible benefits of 'living between two cultures'.

> *Simon* (8:11)   They have different customs – fun customs, like Jewish people (like me) have Chanukah.
> *Zoe* (10:8):   Nice to be black to see the different religions.

One of the more disturbing aspects of talking to our children about 'race' was the extent to which, regardless of their age or social class, they thought of black people as in some sense alien. While this perception was particularly prevalent among the six-year-olds, there was, in their case, no accompanying racist connotation; which is not, of course, to cast doubt on their abilities in this respect. In contrast, the xenophobia of some second and fourth years was quite overt.

> *Ben* (9:4):   [I'd rather be white] because there are more whites in this country and it is meant to be white.
> *Janine* (9:2):   [The worst thing about being black is that] you get picked on. Most people are white so they don't like you. They think blacks should stay in their own country and not come to ours.
> *Steve* (11:2):   You see bad things on the news about black people.
> GS: Such as?
> *Steve*:   Coming over from their own country and overrunning this country.

Quite spontaneously, Laurence (10:8) alerted us to the teacher's role in fostering these ideas.

> GS: Are there any disadvantages in being black?

Laurence: It's harder to get a job because whites have been here longer and [employers] want people from our country, not people who have just come in. Mrs Collins was talking about this this morning. So many people are out of work and now the Indians are starting to come in so there'll soon be more white people unemployed than black 'cos the black are making their own jobs and not employing white people.

We asked the fourth years from Middleton why black people came to this country in the first place. Only one referred to the labour shortage and even he thought the then migrants originated from South Africa and Vietnam! Other 'reasons' for the black presence in Britain included the following:

Their own country was corrupt and had lots of violence.

Some just came to see what it's like and decided to stay.

'Cos the queen owns it and they're part of the Commonwealth and can come to Britain. They want to come to Britain 'cos they're nearer the queen and can be better protected. If they're in Jamaica, they haven't got as much defence.

These comments go some way towards justifying the antiracist intervention that we undertook with children aged between ten and 13 at two 'all white' schools ('Oldtown' junior and Denby Dock middle). The case study is discussed in Chapter 5.

We also inquired from some second and fourth years where people get their ideas about black people. Apart from a couple of second years who claimed they did not know, and another one or two who thought their own imagination responsible, the two groups responded in much the same way. They referred, *inter alia*, to parents, other people (including other children), and direct experience, but most often they mentioned television news. One fourth year also pointed to televised fiction: 'In Rockliffe's Babies the criminals are nearly always coloured people.' Another referred to newspapers, but none considered the role and influence of other forms of literature such as books and magazines.

We concluded our interviews on race by presenting the children with two moral dilemmas. With reference to the blatant racism so widespread in the 1950s and early 1960s, the first was as follows:

> A long time ago in London, you could be walking down the street when you would see a notice in a shop window which said, 'we won't serve black people in this shop'. Do you think that was fair?

Although not a single child thought it was, the reason most often advanced by the six- and seven-year-olds was that 'black people can't get what they want'. However, a few from Middleton were rather more concerned with the grounds for discrimination than with the outcome. They considered it unfair because 'black and white are just the same' or because 'being black doesn't mean anything will happen to the shop'. The overwhelming majority of second years also argued in terms of there being no difference between blacks and whites and while this point of view was represented among the fourth years, many of the latter discussed the issue from the standpoint of equal rights.

The second dilemma dealt with racial discrimination in the workplace.

> One day two people went for a job at a factory; one was black, the other was white. The person who owned the factory said: 'I'll give the job to whoever has the same colour skin as me.' Was that fair?

The single most common response of the infants to this problem was, in a sense, to deny it. They regarded the employer's attitude as unjust because 'he should let both of them do the job'. Thus it would appear that many six- to eight-year-olds do not construe events of this kind as unfair discrimination. In contrast, there was a clear recognition among the second years that skin colour was irrelevant and thus an unjust criterion upon which to base decisions relating to employment. This difference between the two age groups was reflected in their preferred courses of action, for whereas the infants tended to think in terms of giving the job to both applicants, the consensus among the older children was to test them. There was, however, one second year who asserted that the job should be offered to the black candidate because 'it's mainly whites who get jobs so it would be fair if the black person got it for a change'. Although this emphasis on need as well as ability was evident among the fourth years, they were far more inclined to suggest looking at the candidates' exam results, interviewing them or testing them in some other way.

Summary

In exploring the way in which children understand 'race' and racism, it would seem that our second and fourth year juniors possessed similar, and relatively sophisticated ideas, in marked contrast to the top infants. The latter, for example, were in no doubt about the nature and prevalence of individual racism, but unlike their older counterparts, they generally failed to relate their awareness to a broader socioeconomic context. Moreover, as many of our infants had particularly immature views on the origin and biological significance of skin pigmentation, we would question the value of some anti-racist initiatives with children of this age. Our scepticism is reinforced by the apparent inability of so many of the six- to eight-year-olds to comprehend the concept of unfair discrimination. We are not, of course, suggesting that antiracism has no part to play in the infant school, only that any intervention take account of possible cognitive limitations such as those we have highlighted.

Gender

Having been shown pictures of a woman repairing a car with her male companion a mere spectator, the children were initially asked if they had spotted anything unusual. All the fourth years noticed more or less immediately that it was the woman mending a car. The second years, too, were in no doubt as to what was 'wrong', but in three cases (all from Middleton) the role 'reversal' was only commented upon in reply to further probes such as 'Can you see anything else unusual?' There was a similar pattern among the infants where Middleton children, on average, required more questioning than their Workington counterparts before realizing what was 'amiss'. All of them, however, eventually recognized the woman as usurping man's conventional role as machine minder.

The children were then asked to explain why it is that men are more likely than women to repair cars. Among all three age groups the most common replies were that men are stronger, less concerned about their appearance and have more knowledge of technical matters. The youngest children appeared to regard stereotypical behaviour as 'natural', that is, as biologically determined or preordained.

Christopher (6:7): Men are *supposed* to [mend cars] because they're clever and women are *supposed* to do the cooking.
GS: Do you think that women can mend cars as well as men?
Dominic (6:8): No.
GS: Why not?
Dominic: 'Cos they don't know what it's all about.
GS: Why don't they know?
Dominic: 'Cos God made them like that.

The majority of our eight- to ten-year-olds, in common with the younger children, believed that men and women performed distinctive jobs because of differences in strength, knowledge and attitude towards appearance. However, there was a noticeable tendency among the older children (even more pronounced among the fourth years) not only to employ a broader range of psychological 'explanations' for gender divisions within the labour market, but to talk specifically about differences in ability and personality. Interestingly, it was at this age that children first revealed that they had internalized certain racial stereotypes. There was also evidence of a small minority of these eight- to ten-year-olds appreciating that gender inequality in the labour market is not inevitable. This realization was far more evident among the fourth years, especially those at Middleton. A number of them alluded to social constraints when they suggested that women didn't engage in certain types of work because 'it's not thought of' or because 'it's unladylike'. Others referred more directly to the role of the family.

GS: Why do women tend not to fix cars?
Nicholas (11:5): 'Cos they don't like to get themselves dirty.
Neil (11:3): They care too much about their clothes.
GS: Is that true of all women?
Nicholas: Well most women but not all.
GS: Why are women so different?
Nicholas: 'Cos some women have been brought up differently.

While these older children were aware of gender differences in employment, when asked about the provenance of stereotypical notions of occupational role, most were unable to answer or concocted rather bizarre explanations.

GS: Where do we get our ideas from?
Matthew (10:10): Our heads.

GS: Before that?
Matthew: People who made them up like God; people who organise things like the Labour Party, President or Prime Minister.

Overall, the children seemed to know less about the process of stereotyping in relation to gender than in relation to 'race'. A few remarked on the influence of parental precept in reinforcing commonly held conceptions of masculinity and femininity, but only one child mentioned the role of television in shaping these conceptions.

In order to reveal the children's thoughts on the more significant facets of gender differentiation, they were asked to list what they regarded as the 'best' and the 'worst' aspects of life as a boy and as a girl and then to do likewise in relation to men and women. The results showed that six- to eight-year-olds regard boys and girls as differing primarily in terms of their recreational interests, physical skills and attractiveness. Boys were also seen as more troublesome than girls. The failure of the six- and seven-year-olds to comment on the seemingly preferential treatment of boys in school and at home, mirrored their limited understanding of the impact of racism on the lives of many black children in present-day Britain. By comparison, the most significant development among the second years was a widespread recognition that boys and girls are often treated very differently and some awareness that the treatment is often unfair.

GS: What are the worst things about being a boy?
Clive (9:1): It's always ladies first. We haven't done anything wrong so don't see why we should go last. If I had the choice, I'd rather go first.
Nicholas (9:0): If you're hurt, people expect you to be brave. You're expected to be rougher and stronger even though you might not want to be.

By the time children reach the fourth year, a number of them not only realize that boys and girls are treated unfairly by society at large, but believe that individuals in positions of authority may discriminate solely on the basis of gender.

Lee (10:9): A lady teacher picks on boys instead of the girls.
GS: Why?

Lee: 'Cos when she was a girl and was picked on by a man teacher, she now gets her own back.

Nicholas (11:5):   In this school girls are treated more favourably. They don't get told off for talking.

GS: Why does Mrs Collins tell boys off more than girls?

Nicholas :   'Cos Mrs Collins was a girl once.

Andrea (11:2):   When we have apparatus [PE], the boys get to do the good things 'cos the teachers think that girls aren't strong enough.

Louise (11:5):   We're more dainty, but we could do it if we got the chance.

Turning now to consider the children's perceptions of adult gender differences, it is clear that the infants chiefly saw men as more privileged in terms of their leisure opportunities. The fact that only two infants suggested that employment opportunities, overall, may be skewed in favour of men provides a clear parallel with their failure to comment on the marginality of many black men and women in the labour market.

Not surprisingly, as with 'race', the eight- to ten-year-olds seemed to have a rather more sophisticated perception of the adult world. To begin with, a higher proportion of them recognized that employment prospects, *in general*, were brighter for men. When asked to explain this apparent unfairness, the inclination was to blame the victim in the sense of attributing to women either physical or personality defects. They were most frequently portrayed as lacking strength and speed. Thus the tendency to see black inequality in the labour market as a function of racism was not matched by a corresponding inclination to consider the role and influence of sexism. For the most part, the comments of our fourth years differed only in degree from those just described.

We concluded the interviews on gender, as with 'race', by presenting each pair of children with a number of dilemmas relating to unfair discrimination. The first was as follows:

A girl and a boy were sitting on a park bench and they were fighting over a doll – a doll with long hair wearing a dress. The boy wanted to play with it and so did the girl. A grown up came along, stopped the two children from fighting, picked up the doll and gave it to the girl. Do you think the grown up was fair?

The response of our youngest children was almost equally divided between those who thought the adult's reaction to have been just, because boys shouldn't get involved with dolls, and those who thought it unjust because the boy would have nothing to play with. (The importance that so many six- to eight-year-olds apparently attach to the outcome of an event as a determinant of its morality was commented upon earlier when analysing their response to overt racism in public places.)

While roughly half the eight- to ten-year-olds in both schools agreed that boys shouldn't play with dolls, there was a large number (mainly from Middleton) who disapproved of the adult's behaviour on the grounds that 'some boys might want to play with dolls' (cf. Damon, 1977). Compared with the infants, there was very little concern that the girl had been given something and the boy had not.

The most common response among the two groups of fourth years (especially those at Workington) was that boys should not play with dolls. This retreat from the more liberal views of many second years suggests that the age range of eight to ten may prove particularly fertile for teaching children to question gender and other cultural stereotypes.

We next presented the children with a dilemma that again concerned gender stereotyping but which on this occasion involved discrimination against a girl. The findings were essentially the same as in the previous dilemma but with Middleton children, irrespective of age, displaying a more open-minded attitude towards counter stereotypical behaviour.

The final dilemma involved unfair discrimination at work.

A hospital needed a new nurse so it put an advert in the paper. A lady came along and said that she wanted the job, and at the same time, a man came along and said that he wanted it. The people in the hospital thought to themselves: 'Well, nurses are usually women, so we'll give the job to the woman.' Was that fair?

The infants were somewhat divided on this question with those at Middleton once more showing less inclination to think stereotypically. They found it easier to envisage male nurses and were less insistent on men in hospitals having to work as doctors.

Asking the children how the hospital should resolve the issue provided further evidence of the infants' inability to conceptualize unfair discrimination. For the most common response (especially at Middleton) was that both the man and the woman should have been offered the job – full time! Few children suggested that the candidates might share it and only one suggested testing them.

While a handful of second years persisted in the belief that only women could become nurses, the vast majority in both schools thought otherwise. Many also realized that the fairest way to select a candidate was by some sort of test. The trend away from stereotypical judgement in favour of an informed assessment continued among the fourth years, but a number of them drew attention to other considerations. They argued that it might be fairer to offer the job to the man 'as he has a career to think about', 'has to support his family', and 'the lady can always get on with the housework'. On the other hand, one child thought it fairer to give the job to the women because 'men find it easier to get another job'. The tendency of our oldest children to take account of a range of factors was commented upon earlier in the context of employment and 'race'.

Summary

From their response to the above dilemmas, it would appear that six- to eight-year-olds generally equate unfair discrimination with unequal treatment. If one individual is not allowed to do the same as another, that prohibition in itself, no matter how it arose, is seen as unfair. Their preferred solution to problems of distributive justice is to permit everyone who wishes to participate in an activity to do so, for any restriction (such as there being only one job available) is viewed as arbitrary and can thus be disregarded. Older children are markedly less inclined to perceive situations as unfair simply because someone is denied an opportunity that is open to others. In contexts such as we have examined, where justice is in conflict with a cultural stereotype, older children are more likely to think of unfairness in terms of the validity of the stereotype concerned. Hence, it was unethical for the adult to give the doll automatically to the girl, because some boys like playing with dolls.

The notion that some individuals are more deserving than others was almost entirely absent from the remarks of our six- to eight-year-olds, but could be seen in the suggestion made by some of the eight- to ten-year-olds that the hospital ought to test the applicants for the nursing job – a suggestion widely endorsed by the older children.

The observed difference in attitude to gender between the two schools may well have reflected the social class backgrounds of their pupils. The Middleton pupils' less restricted view of gender roles and generally more critical stance towards gender stereotyping was, no doubt, an acknowledgement of the greater autonomy of women in middle class families. (See Carrington *et al.*, 1987, for a review of this literature.)

Class

The pictures shown to the children portrayed the owner of a mansion reprimanding a poor boy and girl for having strayed into the private grounds. Having said what they thought was happening in the 'story', the children were asked why some people are rich and others poor. Whereas the older children tended to focus on occupational status and income level when accounting for differences in wealth, the infants' responses were predictably more naive. As with 'race' and gender, they were more likely to answer tautologically (claiming that 'some people have no money') or by asserting, somewhat unrealistically, that the poor 'had spent it'.

Having given us their explanations for disparities in wealth and income, we inquired next whether the children thought such disparities were fair. The six- to eight-year-olds (working with an absolute concept of poverty) had no doubt that they could not be justified, mainly because the poor would be unable to buy food and other necessities. (There is an obvious similarity here with the same pupils' response to the dilemma involving overt racism in public places.) The older children were more equivocal. Among the second years, differences in wealth were generally considered to be unfair but for no clearly defined reason. For example, it was sometimes just asserted that 'everyone should get the same'. The second years' failure to recognize that some individuals may be more deserving than others has parallels with their views on 'race' where it was thought wrong to prevent the black boy joining in the game 'because black and white are just the same'.

The ten- to 12-year-olds divided slightly more evenly on the question of fairness, but in contrast to the second years, those who regarded poverty as unfair, occasionally provided the following (familiar) rationalizations:

> Gerard (10:6): You can't help being poor if you haven't had good teaching or your parents may not have brought you up properly.
> Trevor (11:3): Everyone deserves to be equal. Poor people might work just as hard.

As with 'race' and gender, we concluded our interviews on social class by presenting the children with various moral dilemmas. The first involved an instance of snobbery.

> One day a young girl asked her mother if she could bring a friend home for tea. 'Is she rich like us or is she poor?' inquired the mother. 'She's poor,' the girl replied. 'Well, in that case,' said her mother 'you cannot bring her home.' Do you think the mother was fair?

Although the response of the infants to this dilemma was varied, a substantial number did not seem to know why the mother behaved as she did, or at any rate could not give a coherent explanation. (We noted the same phenomenon when the infants had been asked if it was fair to stop people joining a game because of their colour.) The second years also raised numerous objections, the most frequent being some variation on the theme that 'money has nothing to do with it.' The oldest children responded in a similar way although they were rather more inclined to talk about 'rich and poor being both the same'. Again the similarities with 'race' are striking.

The second dilemma was as follows:

> Two poor boys were walking down the road and one said to the other, 'do you know, I'd never help the people who live over there.' 'Why not?' asked his friend. 'Because they're rich,' came the reply. Was that a sensible thing to say? Was it fair?

There was very little sympathy for the rich among the infants. They generally thought the boys had acted reasonably because 'the rich don't help the poor' '[and they] can do it for themselves'. These views were also found among the eight- to ten-year-olds, but within this age group there was a very evident concern with reciprocity. In other words, many of them were loathe to generalize and wished to reserve judgement until they knew how the rich had treated the boys. The main difference between the second and the fourth years was a much greater emphasis among the latter on self-interest, i.e., helping the rich for monetary gain.

Finally, we examined the children's thinking about wealth and poverty in the context of employment.

> Two people went for a job in an office. One was rich and very well dressed, the other was poor and very shabbily dressed. Before seeing the two people, the person who owned the office said, 'I'll give the job to whoever is the best dressed.' Was that fair?

In commenting on this dilemma, we see a further manifestation of the difficulty experienced by many six- to eight-year-olds in comprehending the nature of unfair discrimination. They tended to think of the employer as acting unjustly not because a decision was made on the basis of a dubious criterion, but because of the consequences of that decision. They were concerned, for example, because the poor and unsuccessful candidate would be upset. When asked what the employer should have done, most said, 'give it to both'.

In contrast, most of the second years at Workington thought the job should have been offered to the poorly dressed person on the grounds of greater need. At Middleton they also recognized the importance of need, as they had with respect to 'race' and gender, but some were prepared to attach greater weight to the respective abilities of the two candidates and thus suggested testing them. The fourth years from both schools thought the same way as the Middleton second years.

Summary

In the child's developing awareness of social class, it would appear from our study that the age of eight marks a significant turning point. As we have seen, below this age, many of the children failed to provide a plausible explanation for the existence of wealth and poverty, and considered the fairness of wealth distribution in terms of its impact rather than its cause. This particular finding may be thought to corroborate Piaget's (1932) claim that young children, when conceptualizing a misdeed, ignore the underlying intention and consider only the amount of damage. We also noted, in common with the areas of 'race' and gender, that our infants were bereft of any concept of unfair discrimination.

The two older groups of children tended to think about wealth and poverty in similar ways to one another, often expressing ideas and attitudes widely held by adults. However, in relation to unfair discrimination, they were inclined to oppose it, as they were in respect of 'race', on the basis of generalization ('rich and poor are just the same') rather than individual differences (i.e., by stressing that not all people described as either rich or poor are the same).

Overall, we believe that our study has highlighted a number of similarities and differences in the way that children of primary school age tend to think about 'race', gender and social class. We have been principally concerned with the pedagogic implications of our work, for as we have already pointed out, no intervention in the field of political and moral education will succeed with young children unless it takes cognizance of age-related conceptions of structural inequality.

5
Antiracist, Multicultural Education: Some Possible Strategies

In this chapter we appraise various organizational, pedagogical and curricular strategies for antiracist, multicultural education in the primary and middle years of schooling. We show how these can vary in accordance with the social and ethnic composition of the school, the age range of its pupils and its location. We first examine strategies to combat institutional racism, both in 'all white' and in multiracial schools, focusing on organizational factors such as staffing, assessment and referral procedures, grouping, parental involvement and home–school links, and policies to deal with racial incidents. We then consider different pedagogical strategies (peer tutoring, collaborative learning and school exchanges), and look at techniques to democratize the school and classroom environment. Finally, curricular issues, including antiracist teaching, are discussed before we present the findings of a case study undertaken at two 'all white' schools, one primary, the other middle.

Drawing upon this material, we show how children aged between ten and 13 respond to teaching about forms of racism as part of a wider programme of political education. We argue that for such teaching to be effective, steps must be taken to democratize classroom relationships, suggesting that issues of social justice and equality (whether of 'race', gender or class) can only be meaningfully explored where a serious attempt is made to redress the imbalance between teachers and taught. We also illustrate the value of collaborative learning as a means of restricting didacticism, developing empathy and cooperation and facilitating an exchange of ideas.

Organizational strategies

The following discussion is premised upon the contention that the hidden curriculum is as important as the formal curriculum in shaping pupils' attitudes and aspirations. Stereotyped notions of gender role, for example, may be transmitted to pupils in primary and middle schools where men continue to occupy disproportionately positions of authority and control (DES, 1985b). If the structure of the teaching force is an important factor in gender socialization as a result of teachers providing role models (especially for young children) then it would seem reasonable to argue that the ethnic composition of a school's staff is equally important. What message, for example, is conveyed to children by a teaching staff where ethnic minorities are either conspicuous by their absence or by their overrepresentation in low status roles? Concern about this issue has been voiced by various bodies including the Commission for Racial Equality, which has recently reported on a survey of eight multiracial LEAs. It noted that:

> The total number of teachers in the 1,189 schools surveyed was 20,246, of whom only 431 (2%) were of ethnic minority origin. It should be remembered that these schools are in areas where the proportion of people of ethnic minority origin is higher than the national average.
>
> The ethnic minority teachers were disproportionately on the lowest scales. 78% of ethnic minority teachers were on scales 1 or 2 compared with 57% of white teachers. At the other end of the profession, 5% of ethnic minority teachers were deputy head or headteachers compared with 13% of white teachers.
>
> (Commission for Racial Equality, 1986, p. 14)

Schools are clearly limited in their ability to ameliorate this situation while the number of ethnic minority students in training remains so low. (We deal with this issue in greater detail in Chapter 7.) However, schools in multiracial areas should make every effort to redress imbalances within their staffing structures so as to ensure a greater degree of symmetry in ethnic composition between teachers and pupils. While recognizing this as an ideal towards which schools might aspire, we feel that it can be justified on grounds other than those relating to pupil socialization. For example, the inhibitions that minority parents can have in approaching their child's school (Tomlinson, 1984) might be lessened and possibly surmounted. Additionally, such appointments would have the advantage of extending the cultural perspectives of teachers and thus helping to ensure that institutional responses to racism and ethnocentrism are appropriate. If policies to promote racial equality are to operate as effectively as possible, it could be beneficial for some members of staff to share the critical life experiences of ethnic minority pupils and their parents. While the need for ethnic monitoring by LEAs and schools may be more pressing in racially heterogeneous areas, we would stress that appointing bodies in 'all white' areas should show a similar concern. We believe that the implementation of this recommendation would assist in challenging the racism that appears to be prevalent in such areas. As Winifred Mould's (1987) research into the racial attitudes of young people attending exclusively or predominantly white schools has shown, individual racism remains rife within those sections of the white community that lack direct experience of racial minorities and who are not, in the main, competing with them for cultural and economic resources. She reported that 75 per cent of those approached during her research 'held negative attitudes about black people, and of those about one third held strongly hostile attitudes'. A recent investigation by one of us of young South Asians in a northern city (where ethnic minorities formed less than 5 per cent of the overall population) has corroborated Mould's findings. More than three-quarters of the 114 people interviewed were able to recount personal experiences of racism ranging from verbal abuse through to physical violence (Carrington *et al.*, 1987). The youngest of those taking part in the study were aged 11; the oldest were in their early twenties. The racial incidents referred to occurred mostly at school or in the workplace.

Racial incidents

Although many local authorities and individual schools have produced policy statements stressing the need for staff to be vigilant over matters relating to racism and to show no ambiguity in the way in which they react to racist behaviour among pupils, such prescriptions may not always be put into practice. There are indications that the racist motives underlying some acts of aggression, intimidation and verbal abuse can be ignored by teachers. As the work of Dunn (1986), among others, has suggested, teachers tend 'to turn a blind eye' to racist behaviour and are often unwilling to discuss 'race'-related issues in the classroom. As we have already seen, this apparent reluctance to discuss 'race' (or other controversial issues) could be especially pronounced among teachers of young children whose acceptance of idealist conceptions of 'childhood innocence' may prompt them to dismiss racist name-calling and related behaviour as mere childishness. Furthermore, the children may also be seen as intellectually incapable of handling such complex and sensitive matters. There may also be other reasons why teachers fail to respond to such behaviour. For example, policy statements are not always translated into workable guidelines for action. This can present staff with particular problems as a recent investigation into the implementation of an antiracist policy at 'Arkwright High School' has shown (Carrington and Williams, 1988). Several teachers at the school indicated that despite their commitment to the authority's policy on race, they nevertheless experienced difficulties in implementing it. For example, Mr Bennett, a member of the Religious Studies department said:

We need some advice on what to do when things go wrong. Alright, so we monitor a racial incident, but how do we actually handle it? We're told to report it; we're told to do something about it, but what? How do you handle it? I think with many of these antiracist policies, the people who are trying to train others don't know the answers themselves.

At first sight, Jon Nixon (1985) appears to provide Mr Bennett with solutions. He makes suggestions for dealing with children who bring racist literature into school and who are involved in racial abuse, either verbal or physical. Upon further examination, however, Nixon's recommendations are unlikely to assuage Mr Bennett's anxieties, for the advice he dispenses is both vague and arguably naive. In relation to racist literature, for example, teachers are urged to send 'offending pupils... to a senior member of staff' (p. 66). No suggestions though are made as to how matters should then proceed. Nixon further suggests that such literature should be confiscated, but it is our contention that while the school should not want to be seen as legitimating this type of material, there could be problems with the line of action proposed by Nixon. The recent controversy surrounding the publication of Peter Wright's book *Spycatcher* illustrates the point in so far as it shows how the censorship of material can often enhance its appeal.

We agree with Nixon that the crucial role of the home in the formation of racial attitudes must not be overlooked, and that it is essential for schools to contact parents when dealing with racial incidents. But he gives little advice about the form that such counselling might take or about its likely outcomes. In addition, while Nixon is correct in stressing the need for schools to show their abhorrence of racist behaviour, it is unlikely that his seemingly punitive and repressive framework would provide an ethos conducive to the reduction of individual racism. Furthermore, some of his proposals are at variance with the principles of antiracist, multicultural education, that is, an education concerned with equipping young people with the range of skills and dispositions needed to become decent, fairminded, responsible and rational citizens. Surely, any intervention to combat individual racism should be primarily educative rather than repressive if these goals are to be realized. While the expulsion of racist pupils might be viewed by pupils as an ultimate sanction, counselling, because of its essentially educative nature, might be regarded as a preferable interim measure. However, we do not see the solution as simply residing in the re-education of individual racists who just happen to be 'caught'. In the long term, we see the solution to this problem as lying in the model of political and moral education previously described.

Assessment and referral procedures

For many years anxieties have been voiced about the educational performance of Afro-Caribbean children and their overrepresentation in the lower bands and sets of secondary schools (see Tomlinson, 1984). Although there have been studies of ethnic differences in attainment among children of primary age (see Taylor, 1981), there is a dearth of information on ethnic differences in *ability grouping* at this level. Despite this absence, there are indications that setting (and other forms of grouping by ability) is not uncommon in primary and middle schools (Barker-Lunn, 1984; DES, 1983b). Although we recognize that no simple connection can be made between teachers' expectations and their classroom behaviour (Short, 1985), it is certainly conceivable that stereotyped notions of the academic abilities of black pupils could have some influence on their academic placement. For this reason, we urge that primary school teachers, when appraising their allocation and assessment procedures, take account of ascriptive criteria to include class and gender as well as 'race'. The need to scrutinize such procedures will be especially important with the introduction of national attainment tests from the age of seven.

Whole school approaches

A 'whole school' approach to antiracist, multicultural education may help to ensure that a range of practical problems are overcome and viable curricular strategies are developed ('Viability' may depend on a number of factors *including* the level of staff and parental support for the initiative, the pupils' ages and the location and ethnic composition of the school.) A 'whole school' approach, as David Milman's (1984) reflections on the development of a multicultural policy at Childeric Primary School in Deptford has suggested, can have several advantages. First, the collegial and democratic ethos normally associated with such an approach may enable staff to discuss any anxieties or misgivings relating to the policy and its implementation. Secondly, as well as performing an invaluable INSET function, such discussions are essential if the policy is to be continuously monitored and appraised, and changing priorities identified.

Of course, it is not only teaching staff who need to be involved in the formation and development of a policy. In the multiracial school, ancillary staff will need to understand and accept the policy if, for example, racial incidents are to be dealt with in a consistent and uniform manner. It is also necessary that the aims and objectives of the policy are adequately explained to parents for, invariably, understanding is a prior condition of acceptance. Breakdowns in communication can occur, as the staff of Gayhurst Infants School in Hackney found:

When the draft statement was completed, it was taken to the parents for any discussion and amendment they thought was necessary. Generally they were supportive when each point of the policy was discussed. At the end, one parent said, 'It was just as well that it was explained to me because I couldn't understand a bloody word of it.' This made us realise that the policy was very jargonistic, and a group of parents and teachers offered to re-write it in a more understandable form.

(Mulvaney, 1984, p. 29)

As we have argued elsewhere (Carrington and Short, 1989), however carefully an antiracist, multicultural education policy is formulated and packaged, its impact will be minimal unless both children's racial attitudes *and* those of their parents are addressed concomitantly. While we recognize the importance of *intra*-school strategies in combating racism, the crucial role of the home in socialization must not be overlooked. The 'hearts and minds' of parents have to be won over for, while children spend in the region of 15,000 hours *in school*, a further 70,000 hours is spent outside (Heath and Clifford, 1980). There are, however, a number of constraints upon parental consultation and involvement, as Tom Vassen (1986) has pointed out in his appraisal of antiracist, multicultural policies in four London primary schools. He notes:

Lack of involvement has three main stands. First, the unwilling-ness of teachers to participate with parents who are regarded as 'non-professionals' and thereby not qualified to offer anything. Second, the notion that parents' duties cease at the school gate. Third, the schools' rigidity in structuring visits which do not take into account the work commitments of parents.

(Vassen, 1986, p. 131)

He goes on to outline a number of strategies to facilitate better home–school links (p. 132):

(i) establishing a Parents, Teachers and Friends association;

(ii) social functions where parents, teachers and interested parties can mix on an informal basis;

(iii) organising events that encourage various cultural interests;

(iv) parents' evenings planned with flexibility and consultation;

(v) parents with expertise in various skills can be encouraged to work with teachers in classrooms. Cookery, woodwork, art and craft offer suitable opportunities;

(vi) parents talking to children about their occupations and background diversity (religion, traditions, customs);

(vii) establishing a parents' room with library containing examples of children's work as well as reading for adults.

Links with the community

Whereas Afro-Caribbean parents have tended to express dissatisfaction with the quality of their children's academic education, South Asian parents have more often expressed misgivings about the perceived violation of their cultural norms and values in school. Frequently, physical education has provided the focal point for this disquiet. Muslim (and to a lesser degree Sikh) parents often have deeprooted reservations concerning their daughters' participation in this area of school activity, especially in swimming. According to Taylor and Hegarty (1985, pp. 371–2):

> This matter is related to the issue of dress and the potentially dire social consequences, to the point of ruining marriage prospects for a girl and her siblings, if she should be seen by male teachers or boys in such a deshabillé state.

Close links between home and school have long been widely recognized as integral to effective teaching (Mortimore and Blackstone, 1982). We have hinted at a gulf in relations between schools and some ethnic minority parents and turn now to consider possible ways of bridging it. Some of the strategies we discuss were implemented at Arkwright High School in their attempt to extend participation of both white and South Asian girls in curricular and extra-curricular PE.

Many schools, both secondary and primary, are aware of the language barrier in relation to some South Asian parents and take steps to translate all forms of communication whether inside the school or between school and home. When girls at Arkwright began to drop out of extra-curricular activities, the initial response on the part of PE staff was to send letters to their parents. However, 'This approach was often...insufficient, as Mrs Rodgers [a PE teacher] pointed out: "We send letters home asking their parents if they can come and their parents say no".'

It was generally felt among the staff that a more personal touch was required. In Mr Bennett's view:

We need to talk [directly] to parents about the school system and its values. We should go out to them and not expect them to come in to us and ask questions. It must be a very daunting prospect, if you don't know the system, have a working class background and don't have the communication skills needed to come into a big school like ours... It seems the best way of doing things is personal contact. Letters, even if translated, don't have much effect.

A more personal and direct approach may indeed improve relationships between home and school. However, unless such personal contact is handled with sensitivity and with an understanding and sympathy for cultural difference, it could very easily prove counterproductive. The implications for teacher training are self-evident and apply equally to all minority cultures. Additional means of fostering closer links between teachers and ethnic minority parents have included joint parent–teacher working parties and various forms of social gathering often planned as celebrations of cultural diversity. The value of these contacts lies not only in complementing other school-based initiatives aimed at undermining some teachers' erroneous perceptions of minority communities, but in providing a forum for teachers to learn about parental anxieties and an opportunity to allay them where possible. As Tomlinson (1984, p. 41) noted when reflecting on her study of Handsworth schools:

Most teachers, in parallel with most parents interviewed, did hope that multiracial schools would provide a caring, controlled environment for learning, for all pupils, but the teachers did not have sufficient contact and communication with parents to make it clear that they shared this objective.

One of our major concerns throughout this book has been to stress the importance of antiracist, multicultural education in the all white school. However, in making this recommendation, we recognize that parental indifference, or, indeed, active opposition, to such measures may be a far more difficult obstacle to surmount than in multiracial areas. To overcome, or at least to lessen, the opposition, we propose that the incorporation of antiracist, multicultural education be defended in terms of the principles that define a good education. These were outlined and discussed in Chapter 1. All-white schools must be prepared both to communicate and to demonstrate the compatibility of antiracist, multicultural education with a democratic education that seeks to encourage the development of citizens who, among other things, are able to recognize, and willing to act against, all forms of social injustice.

Pedagogical strategies

As various commentators have noted (e.g., Richards, 1986), local authority and school policy statements in antiracist, multicultural education have tended to give insufficient consideration to matters relating to pedagogy and have largely failed to provide unambiguous and workable strategies for the classroom. Notwithstanding this, research has been undertaken, both in Britain and the United States, into various practical approaches which may help to reduce individual racism and promote better interracial and intercultural understanding. It is to this research that we now turn.

Peer tutoring

'Peer tutoring' or 'cross-age tutoring' is one such method. As Carol Fitz-Gibbon (1983) has shown, in a typical peer tutoring project, older pupils are trained to work on a one-to-one basis with younger pupils. Supervised by qualified teachers, the 'tutors' provide instruction on an agreed aspect of the curriculum over a two or three week period. Research has indicated that the technique may

> be one of the most effective interventions yet found for improving achievement, both for tutors and those tutored: tutors learn the work (i.e., subject matter) thoroughly because they have to teach it, and tutees benefit from individual attention.
>
> (Fitz-Gibbon, 1988, p. 160)

Fitz-Gibbon has demonstrated that, during these interventions, tutors and tutees tend to develop 'friendly feelings' towards one another once their 'initial shyness has been overcome.' Citing the work of, among others, Slavin (1979) in the United States, she argues that in the multiracial school, the pairing of pupils from different ethnic backgrounds may help 'break down barriers' and 'produce more positive attitudes and less stereotyping'. Cognizant of the practical constraints on peer tutoring and potential staff resistance to the initiative (especially during a period of financial exigency), she has also suggested that it can have the additional benefit of creating a collaborative rather than competitive ethos in the classroom:

> Direct instruction is not avoided but the atmosphere is changed to one for which many forms of 'alternative education' strive: an atmosphere of active participation, personal efficiency, interaction, cooperation, empathy and enjoyment.
>
> (Fitz-Gibbon, 1983, p. 163)

She goes on to emphasize that peer tutoring can not only contribute to pupils' development as decent citizens, but does so without compromising academic standards:

> Since experiments have repeatedly shown that both tutors and tutees learn more during tutoring sessions (generally indeed they learn more than by direct instruction), one is getting the best of both worlds: *affective goals are achieved while no sacrifice of basic instruction is made.* [Emphasis added.]

While peer tutoring would seem to offer an excellent means of undermining the racial stereotypes of some pupils, it is questionable whether the approach would be as effective with (so-called) 'hard-core' racists.

School exchanges

Exchanges between multiracial and 'all white' schools have also been advocated as a means of combating racism and ethnocentrism among children. Veronica Lee, John Lee and Maggie Pearson (1987) have provided ethnographic data on such an initiative in the South

West of England. They discuss the links that were established between an inter-city primary school (described as 'racially and culturally mixed but almost entirely working class') and a socially heterogeneous 'all white' primary school. A teacher at each school decided that their respective classes would benefit from the opportunity to visit each other and thus mutual visits were arranged. The teachers agreed that, before the visits took place, a considerable amount of preparatory work with the children on stereotyping (by 'race' and gender), racist name-calling and forms of media bias should occur. Following the curricular initiative in antiracist, multicultural education, their classes then met on four occasions: the children from the inner-city school entertained their suburban peers with a Diwali celebration which included a puppet show, and then hosted an urban trail; the suburban school also hosted a trail, set up various problem-solving activities (involving collaboration between children from both schools), and arranged for the children to interview one another.

School exchanges, if not adequately planned and followed up, could be construed as 'tokenistic' and as reinforcing populist conceptions of ethnic minorities (and their culture) as 'exotic' or even 'alien'. Lee and her colleagues are to be commended: their inclusion of the school exchanges within a broader programme of political education helped to obviate these potential dangers.

Collaborative learning

Although collaborative or cooperative learning can take many different forms, the defining characteristic in each case is a mutual dependence among group members in pursuit of a common objective. The theoretical roots of this approach to learning are to be found in the 1950s when experiments were conducted mainly by American social psychologists (Sherif et al., 1954) into variables affecting inter-group relations. These experiments consistently found that whereas competitive activities tend to provoke feelings of hostility between individuals, tasks that can be accomplished successfully only by individuals working together more often result in positive feelings. It is thus no surprise to find that collaborative learning techniques have been employed across a range of settings in a bid to ease racial tensions. In relation to multiracial schools, the impact of collaborative learning has been evaluated recently by Robert Slavin (1983), among others. He notes that providing there is an equality of status among the participants, collaborative techniques not only promote inter-racial friendship but do so, apparently, without impairing academic attainment. Indeed, he claims that collaborative learning increases levels of attainment. James Lynch (1987) goes even further and lists the benefits of cooperative over non-cooperative techniques as follows:

> superior academic learning, achievement and productivity; improved self-esteem; better relationships between pupils of different racial and ethnic backgrounds and between handicapped and non-handicapped pupils; greater mutual concern and trust... Quite unequivocally, teachers may seek to adopt cooperative methods in the knowledge that they are possibly among the most potent approaches for the improvement of race relations.
>
> (Lynch, 1987, p. 133)

While recognizing the value of collaborative learning to the multiracial school, we do not see its benefits restricted to such schools. On the contrary, we believe that collaborative learning is predicated upon the same principles as antiracist, multicultural education. These principles, as we have argued, are compatible with a good education and therefore should be promoted in all schools irrespective of ethnic composition. We claim no originality for this view, for as Allport (1954) noted more than 30 years ago:

> If segregation of the sexes prevails, if authoritarianism and hierarchy dominate the system, the child cannot help but learn that power and status are the dominant factors in human relationships. If, on the other hand, the school system is democratic, if the teacher and child are each respected units, the lesson of respect for the person will easily register. As in society at large, the *structure* of the pedagogical system will blanket, and may negate, the specific intercultural lessons taught.
>
> (Allport, 1954, p. 511)

More recently, Davey (1983, pp. 181–2) has argued along very similar lines:

[Multicultural programmes are] unlikely to have a great deal of influence on peer relationships unless what is taught is in harmony with how it is taught. There is, for example, an exquisite irony in attempting to instruct children in the ideal of some interdependent multi-ethnic society when they are divided by the apartheid of ability groupings or expecting them to appreciate the value of human rights when they are denied freedom of speech.

Purging textbooks of black stereotypes, boosting the minority groups in the teaching materials and adjusting the curriculum to accommodate cultural diversity, will have little impact on how children treat each other, if teachers make rules without explanation, if they command needlessly and assume their authority to be established by convention.

We concur fully with these sentiments but fear that the prevailing sympathy for 'traditional' practice among primary teachers will ensure that collaborative learning remains 'a totally neglected art' (Galton, 1981). As Joan Barker-Lunn's (1984) survey has shown, the vast majority of junior schoolteachers:

prefer a didactic approach rather than a reliance on discovery method, [are making] increasing use of class teaching, continue to emphasise the so-called 'basic' skills of English and maths and are firmly in control of their classrooms.

(Barker-Lunn, 1984, p. 187)

In this type of pedagogical environment, as studies of classroom communication have indicated (e.g., Young, 1984; Edwards and Furlong, 1978) typical exchanges between teachers and pupils follow the characteristic pattern of question-response feedback. Teachers generally dominate 'official' classroom talk, telling pupils 'when to talk, what to talk about, when to stop talking and how well they talked' (Edwards and Furlong, 1978 p. 14). With this pattern of interaction, it is the teacher who (as 'expert' and sole arbiter of truth) transmits a predetermined content to pupils. To facilitate the smooth transmission of knowledge, the teacher invariably presents 'closed' questions to the class, takes the decision about which pupil will answer, provides cues to ensure that pupils make the 'appropriate' responses and do not depart unduly from the lesson's planned trajectory, and constantly evaluates and appraises the responses. In the words of Edwards and Furlong (1978, p.24): 'the transmission of knowledge creates and sustains very unequal communication rights between teachers and learners'. It is our contention that this form of pedagogical relationship, where the status differences between teachers and pupils are accentuated and where only one viewpoint (i.e., the teacher's) is valid, stands in opposition to both antiracist and democratic principles. Indeed, we might ask, could these asymmetrical relations ever provide a basis upon which pupils can meaningfully explore issues relating to social justice and equality, challenge the status quo (whether of race, gender or class), display an open mind, or take a critical stance towards information? As Young has argued, 'the dominant pattern of classroom communication is indoctrinational', in so far as 'it is structured to exclude, repress and prevent the exploration of questions concerning the validity of acts and simple generalisations which make up the bulk of information transmitted in classrooms' (1984, p. 236).

We also fear for the future of collaborative learning as a result of the implementation and monitoring of the National Curriculum. For where teachers' career prospects are contingent upon the test performance of their pupils, the likelihood of experimentation and progressive innovation is not only diminished, but may well suffer at the expense of an increased emphasis on competition and a heavier concentration on the so-called 'core' subjects (DES, 1987).

Many of the strategies outlined here to promote discussion and collaboration and to restrict teachers' domination of classroom talk are especially relevant in multilingual settings. It is to the issue of linguistic diversity that we now turn.

Curriculum issues

Bilingualism and bidialectalism

A multilingual approach should not only be an essential feature of home–school liaison in ethnically-mixed schools, but should also be a major consideration in the development of their antiracist, multicultural curricula. Bilingualism is extensive in contemporary Britain. In many urban centres, bilingual pupils now constitute a sizeable proportion of the school population, e.g., Haringey 30.7 per cent, Waltham Forest 18.8 per cent, Bradford 17.8 per cent, Coventry 14.4 per cent (The Linguistics Minorities Project, 1985, p. 336). As a result of migration to Britain, particularly in the post-war period of economic expansion from the New Commonwealth countries, Cyprus and other parts of Europe, an estimated 131 languages are spoken in ILEA schools, 64 in Bradford and 50 in Coventry. Yet despite this linguistic diversity, the British education system has remained 'dominated by monolingual Anglophones' which, according to Michael Marland (1985, p.124) has ensured that:

> the verbal and written public life of the country excludes the reality of its actual multilingualism. The school system simply has not been led to consider the curriculum implications of our multilingual society or our multilingual world:

Over the years, various attempts have been made to surmount this 'linguistic parochialism'. Conscious of the relationship between language and identity and the ramifications of such ethnocentrism, the Bullock Committee in 1975 urged that every school should:

> adopt a positive attitude towards its pupils' bilingualism and, wherever possible, should help maintain and deepen their knowledge of their mother tongues.
>
> (Bullock Report, 1975, p. 294)

Two years later, this recommendation was reinforced in an EEC directive which urged member states to promote mother-tongue teaching and affirmed the right of ethnic minorities to receive some schooling in their own language and culture (EEC, 1977). Although, more recently, the Swann Committee has acknowledged that schools must (Swann Report, 1985, p. 385) 'both cater for the linguistic needs of the ethnic minority pupils and also take full advantage of the opportunities offered for the education of all pupils by the linguistic diversity of our society today', it offers at best only minimal support for mother-tongue teaching. The Committee stated:

> Mainstream schools should not seek to assume the role of community providers for maintaining ethnic minority community languages... LEAs should offer support for community based

language provision by making school premises available free of charge to community providers, by fostering links between community 'teachers' and the mainstream school, by offering grants for the purchase of books and the development of teaching materials, and by making available to the community their advisory services for short inservice courses.

(Swann Report, 1985, p. 427)

In the absence of unequivocal support for mother-tongue teaching and because of the failure of the DES to provide LEAs and schools with any real leadership in this sphere, it is not surprising that, at secondary level, European languages, especially French, continue to dominate the languages curriculum or, in the primary sector, that the provision of reading materials in languages other than English remains inadequate (Klein, 1985). Furthermore, as Marland (1985, p. 127) has pointed out, 'there is a widespread reluctance to teach in and through mother tongue [because] many parents, governors and teachers have a commonsense worry that learning English is hampered by a "conflicting" mother tongue'. The DES, including the Swann Committee, has done little to counter such beliefs. It is Marland's contention that, as a result, 'virtually no schools have whole curriculum language policies'. To obviate this shortcoming, Marland makes a number of recommendations for primary and secondary schools. For example, to change attitudes, both to bilingualism and to non-European languages, he advocates that school publications, community evenings, assemblies and library stock are multilingual. He also argues that library books, in languages other than English, should 'be integrated and not relegated to an "ESL" corner'. At secondary level, he suggests that the modern languages curriculum needs to be broadened to include (examinable) non-European languages, which would be available to all pupils irrespective of their background. Whereas the bulk of community languages provision in secondary schools would be met through optional courses, such teaching in the primary sector could, in Marland's view, 'easily take place alongside the continuing class-teacher curriculum'. In common with other commentators (e.g., Arora 1986b), he maintains that provision in English as a second language (ESL) should not be annexed, but should be made available 'across the curriculum', and at all stages during the bilingual pupil's educational career.

Ranjit Arora (1986b) has also made some similar observations about the role of ESL teaching. Focusing on the primary and middle school, she defends the present emphasis on integrated, rather than separate, ESL provision on the grounds that English mother-tongue speakers provide 'powerful' role models for the ESL learner. The ESL teacher working both with ESL learners and other teaching staff in the mainstream classroom, can also help to overcome the stigma and marginality which often accompanies separation and exclusion. It is Arora's contention that ESL teaching:

> is best done through fully integrated project work where language development equals language use within a normal school learning situation, but where appropriate language support through intervention is available as and when necessary. Such teaching should aim towards genuine language use by focusing on *meaning* rather than on correct form. (Emphasis added)
>
> (Arora, 1986b, p. 114)

Among other things, she stresses the need for greater collaboration between ESL and mainsteam staff when: the language demands of specific educational tasks are assessed, materials are examined for racist/sexist bias, worksheets and texts are adapted and made more accessible to ESL learners and language skill profiles are compiled.

The multilingual classroom

In her book, *Language in Multicultural Classrooms*, Viv Edwards (1983) proposes various strategies for teaching bilingual and bidialectal children. She focuses on the importance of classroom talk and stresses the need for teachers to foster communicative competence in their pupils. In respect of this objective, she criticizes the traditional lack of symmetry between teacher and taught and argues that collaborative learning groups are more likely to enhance both the quantity and quality of class discussion. Such groups presumably encourage participants to engage with one another by removing the threat of adult censure and the fear of a large audience. According to Saunders (1982) they also provide opportunities for 'exploring ideas, interpreting information, hypothesising, evaluating, arguing, challenging, disagreeing [and for using] language tentatively, specu-latively and exploratorily'.

The role of storytelling (involving parents in the classroom) is another issue that Edwards (1983) addresses when discussing strategies to promote talk. She notes that South Asian and other bilingual parents have tended to work with small groups of children from within their own communities while Afro-Caribbean parents have been used to tell stories to a whole class or to mixed groups of children. Among the advantages claimed for this form of parental involvement are that:

> ethnic minority adults are seen by all children to be in a position of authority and respect in the classroom. Minority children thus have access to a wider range of roles of adult figures on which to model themselves and indigenous children realise that ethnic minority adults can fulfil the same range of roles as... white people.
>
> (Edwards, 1983, p. 92)

One of the more contentious issues in learning to speak a second language concerns the role of 'correction'. Edwards doubts whether such intervention is 'any more efficacious for the second language learner than it is for the young child' and asserts that children start using correct grammar spontaneously rather than in response to adult exhortation. However, the existence of interlanguage (Selin-ker, 1972), in which aspects of a child's mother tongue fossilize and interfere with the acquisition of a second language, would seem to indicate a need for some form of teacher involvement. In support of this point of view, Corder (1974) draws a distinction between random errors resulting from 'chance' factors, such as fatigue, and rule-governed errors that are systematic and reflect the speaker's level of transitional competence. Saunders (1982) suggests that teachers should correct only the latter and that this is best achieved by presenting pupils with opportunities to test hypotheses rather than by providing them straight away with answers. The real issue, therefore, may have less to do with whether teachers should intervene to correct grammatical mistakes than with the form that such intervention should take.

Edwards also makes a number of recommendations in relation to children's reading. Although the advice is particularly valuable for dialect and second language speakers, it clearly has relevance for all children regardless of linguistic status. Her suggestions reflect the importance of reading for meaning rather than accuracy. Thus the favoured strategies include reading aloud which enables children to be questioned 'in order to establish whether they have understood key words or concepts'. Likewise, she is opposed to unnecessarily interrupting the reading process for fear that it will encourage an excessive concern with precise decoding. The problem of over-correction would seem especially serious with regard to dialect-based miscues where the child has, in fact understood the meaning of the text. According to Berdan (1981, p. 220) the impact of teacher intervention in such cases would be that:

> Children learn to cope by reading slower so that they will encounter fewer possible interruptions, by reading at a barely audible level so that teachers cannot determine exactly what was said or simply by refusing to read at all.

The emphasis on meaning is again evident in Edward's advocacy of both Cloze procedure and a related exercise in which 'a frequently recurring unknown or nonsense word, significant to the meaning, is inserted in the text'. Children involved in this latter activity discuss the cues in the text that they use in trying to make sense of the inserted words.

The importance of relevance in reading material is difficult to overstate and Edwards warns of the difficulties that working-class and ethnic minority children may experience in identifying with the 'suburban-semi-detached' world depicted in many reading schemes. She acknowledges recent efforts to overcome this problem and also notes the increased number of novels that 'reflect the multiracial and multicultural composition of present day Britain'. As evidence of the value of culturally relevant material, she cites studies by Grant (e.g., 1973) on the improved reading standards of black American children.

Finally, we consider Edwards' ideas on children's writing: an area largely devoid of research, especially in relation to dialect and second language speakers. She begins by discussing prevailing attitudes towards non-standard features in children's writing and warns teachers against equating such features with poor content. Particular concern is targeted at the over-zealous 'teacher who constantly criticises and "corrects" [and may thus] be perceived as rejecting the dialect speaker's culture and values'. Technical weaknesses in children's writing have obviously to be addressed but Edwards advises that, for most children, this is best done in the last few years of schooling. One reason for leaving it this late is that pupils will be better motivated because of the imminence of their exams.

As far as bilingual children are concerned, Edwards once again points to the dangers in paying undue attention to form at the expense of the content:

> Children progress unevenly and at their own pace towards the target language and the only effect which correction of all the second language learning errors in a piece of writing is likely to achieve is confusion and demoralisation.
>
> (Edwards, 1983, p.126)

Teachers are urged to note and monitor recurring errors and to evaluate 'children's writing by wider criteria than simply its nearness to standard English'. At a more general level, she criticizes the serious shortage of written models (i.e., texts written in an ethnic minority language) to be found in British schools and believes that minority children should be allowed, when appropriate, to write in their own language or dialect. Edwards observes that teachers tend to 'shy away' from initiatives of this kind doubting perhaps their educational value. However, as she goes on to make clear (p. 131):

> Producing children who are literate in standard English... depends on children who have a well-developed sense of them- selves as writers. Attempts to draw on their linguistic skills are likely to contribute to this sense; the devaluation of their skills is likely to produce the opposite effect.

Books and materials

Although various writers have drawn attention to the racism and ethnocentrism of some school texts and teaching materials, showing how black people and non-European cultures are variously ignored, undervalued or presented in a pejorative light (e.g., Hicks, 1981; Gill 1983), it is not proposed to consider this issue at any length.

Notwithstanding this, however, we would like to endorse some of Gillian Klein's (1986) suggestions and stress that initiatives in antiracist, multicultural education require appropriate library and other back-up resources. To ensure that 'the library appears welcoming and relevant to all of the school population, whatever their race, religion, language or class' (p. 169), she advocates, among other things, the use of bilingual labels and posters, and the inclusion of books and periodicals which reflect the cultures, languages and concerns of the *local* community. Klein's remarks about censorship and selection are especially germane, not only to antiracist, multicultural education, but also to other aspects of political and moral education. She points out that:

> While teachers, arguably, can use *any* materials in the classroom, including the overtly racist and sexist, as long as they are sensitive to the messages and can challenge them as they arise – otherwise they appear to condone them – the librarian has to be more rigorous about what she puts on the open library shelves. And certainly this is especially true for young children, who haven't yet been trained towards a healthy scepticism and confidence in their own judgement.
>
> (Klein, 1986, p. 174)

Permeation

Although much has been written and said about the need for schools to eschew 'additive' approaches to antiracist, multicultural education and opt instead for 'permeation', few commentators have gone beyond enunciating the principles upon which a 'permeated' curriculum would be based. There have been relatively few attempts to evaluate the formation and implementation of these policies, particularly in primary schools. This dearth of material is especially incongruous when one considers Richard Willey's (1984b, p. 63) observations about 'permeation':

> Permeating teaching with opposition to racism and with positive responses to ethnic diversity is difficult to approach, complex to work out and taxing to implement.

He goes on to argue (pp. 69–70) that at school and departmental level:

> Complex educational questions arise for teachers to which the rhetoric of official policy provides no readily applicable answers. Difficult decisions have to be made, for example, about the degree and nature of the diversity which the school should encourage and endorse and the relationship of this to the need to provide pupils with the knowledge and understanding which they require to operate in the world outside school. It is at classroom level in multiracial schools that the divergence between pluralist ideals and the realities of contemporary society have to be confronted. Teachers are faced by the need to consider how 'multiculturalism' can be made a rational educational ideology in a society whose institutions are not geared to tolerant pluralism ... Vague injunctions from policy makers about harmony and mutual tolerance have to be translated into rigorous, professional curricular approaches to racism.

Of course, this mismatch between teachers' and pupils' perspectives on race and ethnicity is not only confined to the multiracial school, as our case study below illustrates. However, a cursory examination of the literature reveals that there is much substance in Willey's strictures about policy makers' 'vague injunctions'.

The Swann Report (1985), for example, is replete with such injunctions. Having argued that the curriculum in all schools 'must be permeated by a genuine pluralist perspective which should inform and influence both the selection and the content of the teaching materials used' (p.237), the Committee then provides a list of general criteria which might be employed in evaluation. The disclaimer made by the Committee in its preamble to the checklist, that 'we are not so much concerned with changing the content of the curriculum as with bringing about a reorientation of the attitudes which inform and condition the selection of teaching materials and the way in which various topics are approached and presented' (p. 328), is no doubt an acknowledgement that 'permeation is complex to work out and taxing to implement'. The criteria are as follows:

The variety of social, cultural and ethnic groups and a perspective of the world should be evident in visuals, stories, conversation and information.

People from social, cultural and ethnic groups should be presented as individuals with every human attribute.

Cultures should be empathetically described in their own terms and not judged against some notion of 'ethnocentric' or 'Eurocentric' culture.

The curriculum should include accurate information on racial and cultural differences and similarities.

All children should be encouraged to see the cultural diversity of our society in a positive light.

The issue of racism, at both institutional and individual level, should be considered openly and efforts made to counter it.

Schools have continued to experience various difficulties in presenting cultural diversity in 'a positive light'. The distinction between an empathetic and realistic portrayal of different lifestyles, customs and values, and a treatment of other cultures as 'exotic' and 'strange', may not always be readily appreciated by practitioners. In addition, as Mike Mulvaney (1984, p. 28) has pointed out, when criticizing the 'folksy tokenism' which has been (and possibly remains) widespread in the primary sector, there are enormous 'spin offs' in this approach:

The 'minority' parents turn out to provide food, costumes, artefacts, etc, and appear to be externally grateful. At the end of all such events, staff and parents say 'namaste' to each other, and the school reverts to its celebration of white, male, middle class experience. The parents return to their own experience.

While we accept Mulvaney's observations about tokenism and social control and recognize that this type of curricular initiative can reinforce racial and ethnic stereotypes, we would nevertheless stress that some teaching about cultural difference is essential if children's existing misconceptions are to be effectively challenged (Francis, 1984).

Racism and the primary curriculum

Little is known about how children respond to teaching about race and racism in the primary school. For this reason, the work of Martin Francis (1984), Celia Burgess (1986) and Philip Cohen (1987) warrant particular attention.

Drawing upon his experience as a teacher in a multiracial primary school in south London, Francis has emphasized that antiracist teaching is best undertaken in an environment where discussion, exchange of ideas and openness are encouraged. In his view, environmental studies (especially history), language work and drama are among the most suitable areas of the curriculum for addressing the issue of racism at primary level. Working with fourth year juniors, he has argued that such teaching should begin with the personal experiences of the children concerned, and then progress to a consideration of wider issues: local, national and international. The example he provides is that of a project which started with a discussion of racist abuse at his school, then proceeded to examine press coverage of the New Cross Fire and finally explored aspects of the contemporary black experience in South Africa and the Caribbean. The summative evaluation of the project revealed that one member of the class (who had previously flaunted his National Front sympathies) underwent a change of attitude and severed all connections with the organization.

In common with Francis and other writers on the teaching of controversial issues in the primary and middle years (e.g., Harwood, 1985), Burgess (1986, p. 135) has stressed that political education should not be conceived as 'an abstract intellectual exercise', but should relate initially to the child's direct experience. Working with children aged between six and ten in several multiracial primary schools, she has described how oral and written history, biographies and children's fiction can be used to broach issues relating to both racism and sexism. For example, the life and times of Mary Seacole (a black nurse who worked alongside Florence Nightingale in the Crimea) was employed by Burgess in an attempt to draw parallels with facets of contemporary racism. Although the children were made aware of racial bias in literature and also given some insight into the effects of individual racism, a number of important issues were either glossed over or ignored completely. For example, no reference was made to racism in the labour market, housing or education and, arguably, white children were not provided with sufficient opportunities to empathize with black people.

One of the few accounts of an antiracist initiative conducted in an 'all white' setting has recently been reported by Cohen (1987). He worked with a group of ten- to eleven-year-olds, some of whom were drawn from a 'highly insular white working class' school in an old dockland area. Realizing that 'the polarization between antiracist and multicultural positions had become sterile and self-destructive', he set out to 'develop' and evaluate a cultural studies model of prejudice reduction' which incorporated the best aspects of both. In view of our earlier comments regarding the importance of a holistic approach, it is worth noting that Cohen does not restrict his concern to questions of 'race' but considers various forms of discrimination, including anti-semitism and anti-Irish prejudice. He draws a parallel between the situation that Jewish people faced at the turn of the century and the range of impediments that currently frustrate the black community. This kind of background information is arguably essential if white children are to understand and empathize with their black peers. Thus, in our own work, described below, we attach a high priority to the historical context of contemporary racism.

The case study

Our antiracist initiative was undertaken in two 'all white' schools, Oldtown Primary and Denby Dock Middle, during 1986 and 1987 (pseudonyms are employed throughout the study). Although the teaching programme covered various forms of discrimination, we were particularly interested in children's knowledge of racial and ethnic inequality. Aware of the apparent reluctance of staff in this sector to broach contentious issues in the classroom we were also concerned to present teachers with an example of a practical intervention in political education which would help to allay their apprehensions. The project was initially carried out at Oldtown as part of the normal curriculum of a fourth year junior class of ten- to 11-year-olds. At the time, Geoffrey Short was the class teacher, and Bruce Carrington visited the school as a participant observer. (For a full report of the study, see Short and Carrington, 1987.) Subsequently, a modified version of the project was presented to a third year lower set and a fourth year upper set at Denby Dock Middle school. These children were aged between 11 and 12 and 12 and 13 respectively. On this occasion, Bruce Carrington collaborated with the Head of English and together they devised and implemented a programme tailored to fit in with the existing English curriculum. These revisions reflected the constraints imposed by specialist teaching and setting within the upper school.

At the time of the project, Oldtown Primary was an SPA school located in the heart of a mining area. It served a community with levels of adult and youth unemployment well above the national average. While relationships between members of staff (including the head) and between staff and children were generally relaxed, there was little about the school that would merit the epithet 'progressive'. Despite the bonhomie of the staffroom and the accessibility of the head, there was no evidence of coordinated initiatives in any sphere of the curriculum. Race was no exception, although it should be noted that one or two members of staff had made modest concessions to cultural pluralism in their teaching. (The children involved in our project, for example, had been acquainted with some of the tenets of the world's major religions.)

Denby Dock was a four form entry nine to 13 middle school in a 'respectable' working-class urban area. As in Oldtown, unemployment was high with most job losses in recent years coming in the shipbuilding industry. In common with the majority of nine to 13 middle schools (e.g., DES, 1983b), Denby Dock utilized a mixture of class and specialist teaching. In the third and fourth years where the evaluation was undertaken, the children were set for the high status curriculum areas (such as English and maths) and were taught almost exclusively by specialists. Despite what many primary teachers might regard as a traditional ethos, a number of interesting innovations had occurred. For example, the Head of English, with whom Bruce Carrington worked, was especially interested in developing strategies to promote classroom talk and had experimented extensively with collaborative learning techniques. She was also interested in aspects of media education and, before embarking on the project described below, had done work with both the third and the fourth years in this area.

The project – In living memory

Our commitment to a holistic perspective led us to introduce the project as part of a wider programme dealing with changes in popular culture and lifestyle since the Second World War. The project began with the immediate experiences of the children and members of their family. Parents and grandparents were asked about the jobs they had had during the course of their working lives and their recollections were subsequently examined in the context of changing patterns of employment since 1945. Among the tasks we then set the class was to consider, in small collaborative groups, how they would have solved the acute labour shortage facing the country at the end of the war. It was this activity which led quite naturally into the area of 'race' and immigration for, in every group, one proposed solution was to attract workers from overseas.

> *Jenny* (age 11): We could solve [the labour shortage] by getting the people who emigrated to come back and work in the old jobs. Ask people from an over-populated country such as China and let them work here.
> *Kevin* (11): If I was the government, I would move businesses to other countries or bring other workers from America and all over the world, give them free accommodation and free board...

By making no direct reference to the New Commonwealth, these representative comments suggest that the class initially failed to appreciate the racial dimension of post-war labour migration. (In this respect, we note a close parallel with the fourth years at Middleton – see Chapter 4 – who had little knowledge of why black people first came to Britain in large numbers.) It is for this reason that while acknowledging the contribution of European workers to Britain's post-war economic reconstruction, we explored in greater depth, the nature and experience of the migration from the West Indies and the Indian subcontinent. We were particularly keen to undermine the myth that immigrants from these countries were a cause of unemployment and to this end we made use of archive material illustrating London Transport's recruitment drive in the West Indies.

We provided the children with background information on the sending countries, the scale and timing of the migration and the chief areas of settlement in Britain. However, we were principally concerned at this stage with the children's untutored 'knowledge' of racism (especially its impact on immigrants in the 1940s and 1950s), and we thus gave them the following task. They were to imagine that they had recently entered Britain from either the West Indies or the subcontinent and were writing a letter 'home' to a close relative or a good friend who was thinking of joining them. In these letters, various references were made to manifestations of racial violence, racist name-calling and discriminatory practices in both the housing and labour markets. The following extracts not only typify the concerns expressed by the children in our two schools, but in relation to our findings in Chapter 4, they may well typify ten- to 11-year-olds across the country.

> *John* (11):   . . . you go from house to house trying to get a place to spend the night. Just guess what their reply was after me begging for a bed. It was 'sorry, it's already been took' or just a simple 'no, get lost. We don't give rooms to niggers like you. . . And what about the jobs that you said were very good for someone like me? Oh, I got a job alright. It was a dishwasher in a rotten old fish and chip shop. . .
>
> *Clare* (11):   . . . I advise you to stay at home and forget about Britain. The other day I decided to start looking for a job. As you know, I have plenty of skills. I thought even if nobody likes me, I'll be sure to get a good decent job but I was wrong. Instead I got an awful job cleaning toilets. Over here, that's all they seem to think we're good for. . .

The children only alluded to problems of a cultural nature when discussing their experience of British food.

> *Cheryl* (11):   And the food is just horrible. They eat Baked Beans instead of horse meat and chips instead of raw bean shoots.
>
> *Darren* (11):   The food is different like they don't eat rice as much as us.

While the 12- to 13-year-olds articulated a similarly restricted concept of culture, they seemed to possess a more sophisticated understanding of individual racism. Specifically, they realized that not all white people are prejudiced and that those who are will not necessarily make it obvious.

> *Victoria* (12):   The people who work with me are very nice . . . but the public are horrible however. They throw things at me, spit at me and call me names.

Kerry (12):   I get on well with the people at work but not so much with other people. They think that because I come from India, I shouldn't be allowed to have the job I've got.

Paula (12):   I work on the busses [and get] looks and words behind my back.

In drawing the session to a close, the children were given an opportunity to compare their own piece of writing with black autobiographical accounts of the period (see Husband, 1982).

The activity which followed was an attempt to show the children that British born Afro-Caribbeans and Asians face many of the difficulties which had earlier confronted their parents and grand-parents. The task was modelled on Nixon's (1985) 'direct approach' to racism awareness teaching which, ideally, involves presenting the children with a clearly defined situation and a central character with whom they can identify. The class then engage in small group discussion in order to deal with problematic aspects of the situation. Nixon asserts that:

> The one essential requirement governing [use of the direct approach] is that the teacher should have achieved a good working relationship with the group and that the pupils should be capable of sustaining frank and open discussions with one another
>
> (Nixon, 1985, p. 76)

With our commitment to redressing the unequal communication rights between teachers and learners, every effort was made to meet this condition. The actual cameo read to the children was as follows:

> You are playing in the street where you live when a pantechnicon draws up and unloads. Mr Taylor, a lorry driver from Birming-ham, gets out. He says he's got a couple of 11-year-old twins and he wants advice about this school. What will you tell him?

Almost as an afterthought, the researcher then added:

> Oh, by the way, the family is black, from the West Indies, but the kids were born in England.

At both schools, the children considered their response in small groups before pooling their ideas in a plenary session. On each occasion, one of the more interesting aspects of the class discussion was the length of time that elapsed before any reference was made to 'race'. We do not know whether such reticence reflects the children's view of 'race' as an improper subject for public discourse or whether children in 'all white' areas just do not, under 'normal' circumstances, construe their world in terms of 'race'. The latter is perhaps the more likely explanation in view of the clamour to express an opinion following John's remark:

> *John* (11):   I wouldn't count on anyone liking your kids.
> GS: What do you mean?
> *John* :   They'll be black and everyone else in the school's got a different colour skin.

A number of interesting points emerged from this discussion with a group of 11- to 12-year-olds. First, the children seemed to have internalized the language and logic of racist discourse which, *inter alia*, defines black people as in some sense alien. Liz, for example, said: 'I think the reason why white children won't play with them is ... that they like different types of things.' Another child attempted to legitimate racism in Britain by referring to 'white people getting beat up in Africa'. Rather than perceive such comments as a form of embryonic racism, primary teachers committed to the notion of childhood innocence may well see them as confirmation that primary age children are intellectually incapable of benefiting from teaching about race and other controversial issues. However, opposed to this interpretation, and the argument for non-intervention to which it gives rise, a number of children displayed relatively sophisticated insights. It was recognized, for example, that black youngsters will often get picked on and physically threatened by their white peers; that teachers may perceive them as trouble makers (cf. Rampton Report, 1981); that white people cannot, in terms of their racial attitudes, be treated as a monolithic entity and that skin colour is not necessarily associated with any particular personality trait. Most importantly, perhaps, there was evidence that some of our 11- to 12-year-olds were able to consider racism from the standpoint of the victim. Terry, for example, wrote:

> If I was playing with a black person and a white person came up and called them names, I'd say what do you think you'd feel like if you moved away and had to go to a school where there was a lot of coloured children?

Not surprisingly, the children's written work on 'The Taylor Twins' First Day at School' reflected many of the themes mentioned in the class discussion. There was a widespread emphasis on individual racism but also a realization that not all white people succumb to it. While a number of children in their writing made clear their opposition to racism, only one, an 11-year-old, drew attention to the limitations of assimilation as a means of combatting it.

> One day I went to my new school. My mum also changed my name to Sherry. I thought every body was kind except a boy called Darrin. He was a horrible boy who kept on calling me black Sambo, chocolate biscuit or Sherry coca cola. (Susan: 3rd year Denby Dock.)

When comparing the ideas and attitudes of the two age groups, it was apparent that the chief difference was a more pronounced tendency among the older children to accept the Taylor twins as British. Thus, while Kathy, aged 11, had written:

> The children's names were Saria and Tariq... When [the class] were doing geography, the twins answered all the questions.

Janet, a 12-year-old, commented:

> [Mr Taylor] told me he had two children who were born in Birmingham... All I wanted to know was what are they called... When I plucked up courage to ask, he told me that they are called Sandra and Derek.

We now turn to the final part of our case study which was based on Bernard Ashley's (1975) novel *The Trouble with Donovan Croft*. The children at Denby Dock read it for themselves; those at Oldtown listened to it. The book was considered appropriate largely on account of its realistic portrayal of life in a multiracial junior school and in the surrounding community. It was also thought suitable because of its non-tokenistic treatment of the black characters, its optimistic message with regard to racial tolerance and the ease with which the children could identify with Donovan and his white friend because of the similarity in age.

All the 11-year-olds seemed to enjoy the book, partly because of the suspense.

> *Patsy* : When Donovan started talking the whole classroom just went up and everyone was hoping and hoping for Donovan to talk.
> *Sarah*: I enjoyed it. I thought it was good with a black person instead of a white person.
> *Kathy*: It was good because it explained his feelings.

The 12-year-olds at Denby Dock also reacted very favourably. Vicky's comment was representative:

> I thought it was an interesting book on an important subject. The subject of black and white people living together peacefully. I think it portrays the feelings of the people involved very well. It showed well the problems you can have if a coloured person is living in your house. You could be subject to racist attacks or, as in the story, your neighbour could turn against you.
>
> Donovan was scared when he came to live in England. He had every right to be... I think other pupils will enjoy reading it because it tells them what coloured people feel like when they are being teased.

Summary

As we pointed out in Chapter 1, it is naive to expect direct forms of antiracist teaching to have a beneficial impact upon *all* children. For clearly, those with a psychological need to hate or otherwise disparage an out-group are impervious to reason and thus immune from any such intervention. Nor do we underestimate the influence of structural constraints in undermining egalitarian initiatives in education. However, Gordon Allport (1954, p. 506), while also recognizing these difficulties, does not see them as insuperable.

> the structural view may lead both to false psychology and to false pessimism. It really is not sensible to say that before we change personal attitudes we must change total structure; for in part, at

least, the structure is the product of the attitudes of many single people. Change must begin somewhere. Indeed, according to the structural theory, it may start *anywhere*, for every system is to some extent altered by the change in any of its parts.

Although researchers are currently far from discovering the best means of changing children's racial attitudes, the provision of correct information, especially where it challenges false stereotypes, as in our own case study, should not be undervalued. In support of this view Allport (p. 486) urged antiracists: 'to resist the irrational position that invites us to abandon entirely the traditional ideas and methods of formal education'.

6
In the Wake of the Swann Report: Current Controversies and Dilemmas

After much delay, the Swann Report (*Education for All*) was finally published in March 1985. According to Bhikhu Parekh (1985, p. 4), it was primarily concerned with three issues:

> First, is it the case that some groups of children systematically underachieve in our schools, defining underachievement in terms of the generally accepted criteria of examination results? Second, if they are, what are the reasons? And third, what can and should we do to help them... within the specific context of the prevailing education system?

Swann's analysis and prescriptions in respect of the above elicited a predictably hostile response from the political Right (e.g., Honeyford, 1987). More surprisingly, perhaps, the Committee's recommendations also generated considerable opposition among those on the Left committed to redressing racial inequalities in education. The latter (e.g., Naguib, 1985; Troyna, 1986) have been particularly critical of sections of the Report dealing with ethnic differences in attainment, the teaching of community languages and the debate over separate schools. As we considered the issue of language when discussing curricular strategies to promote antiracist teaching, we will restrict our concern in the present chapter to the two remaining areas of major controversy.

The past couple of decades, as previously pointed out, have witnessed continuing unease at the scholastic performance of Afro-

Caribbean children. Numerous studies since the early 1960s have suggested that they tend to achieve less well than children from other ethnic groups at both primary and secondary level, and are disproportionately represented in lower streams, remedial groups and special schools. (See Taylor, 1981; Tomlinson, 1983; and Figueroa, 1984, for comprehensive reviews of the relevant literature). In the first part of this chapter, we consider ethnic differences in attainment and examine whether Afro-Caribbean pupils do, in fact, 'underachieve'. Possible directions for future research in this contentious and vexed area are then discussed before we move on to evaluate the role of teacher expectation as a cause of the alleged underachievement and the value of voluntary (or supplementary) schools as a response to it. We conclude the chapter by looking at some of the major concerns currently facing the South Asian communities which have prompted demands for the setting up of separate, voluntary-aided schools.

The nature of underachievement

Robert Jeffcoate (1984) makes clear that when we talk about Afro-Caribbean 'underachievement', we mean that such children, *on average*, attain lower scores on a range of tests (including public examinations) than children from other ethnic groups, assuming the same distribution of ability within each group. The Swann Committee recognized that doubt persists in some quarters as to whether this assumption is, in fact, valid. It noted:

> Our interim report was criticised (partly because) it failed to consider IQ, held by many to be responsible for West Indian underachievement...
>
> (Swann Report, 1985, p. 81)

Consequently, a research paper was commissioned from Nicholas Mackintosh and C. Mascie-Taylor. They found that:

> The often quoted gap between West Indian and white IQ is sharply reduced when account is taken of socio-economic factors – contrary to general belief, IQ scores, like school performance, are related to these factors.
>
> (Swann Report, 1985, p. 81)

The Swann Committee believed that Mackintosh and Mascie-Taylor had effectively 'disposed of the idea that West Indian underachievement can be explained away by reference to IQ scores' (p. 71). This was a conclusion that seems to have prompted some, including the Committee itself, to search for more convincing explanations, but others have remained sceptical, doubting the very existence of the problem. They ask whether children of Afro-Caribbean origin can fairly be said to perform less well, especially in public examinations, than other children.

The evidence

The Rampton Committee (Rampton Report, 1981) reported the findings of the 1978/1979 DES School Leavers Survey in six LEAs with high concentrations of children from the ethnic minorities. They claimed that in terms of CSE grade 1, 'O' and 'A' level results, 'West Indian' children, overall, performed substantially less well than both 'Asians' and 'All Other Leavers'. (With the exception of English language, 'Asian' children seemed to be doing more or less as well as 'All Other Leavers'.) Although the Swann Committee, using data from five of the original six LEAs, noted a 'statistically significant' improvement in the relative performance of 'West Indian' children, they confirmed Rampton's findings that (p. 64) 'Asian leavers (were) achieving very much on a par with... their school fellows from all other groups in the same LEAs.' The exception, once again, was English language.

As major documentary landmarks, the findings from both the Rampton and Swann Reports were subjected to considerable media coverage. While some might have considered the publicity justified, in terms of the supportive evidence from a plethora of less well known studies, others were somewhat reluctant to accept the research at face value. They did not so much dispute the evidence, as question its interpretation.

Frank Reeves and Mel Chevannes (1981), for instance, pointed out that Rampton totally ignored social class variables when comparing the school leaving qualifications of the three groups of children. At that time, the Afro-Caribbean community was, as it remains, predominantly working class in contrast to the socially more heterogeneous South Asian and indigenous white communities. Since the link between socioeconomic status and academic attainment is well known (e.g., Halsey *et al.*, 1980), Reeves and

Chevannes maintained that: 'the statistical data, in the form in which they are presented, are insufficient to support the assertion of [Afro-Caribbean] underachievement' (p. 39). The Swann Committee acknowledged the methodological limitations of its interim data, but none the less felt compelled to reproduce the exercise in 1981/2. Its findings are therefore vulnerable to the same criticism. In fairness, however, it should be pointed out that research which *has* taken account of social class variables tends to confirm the relatively low attainment levels of this ethnic group. The ILEA Literacy Survey (Mabey, 1981), for instance, claimed that the standard of reading among Afro-Caribbean children could not 'be entirely explained by differences in social factors', and the National Child Development Study (with its admittedly small sample of Afro-Caribbeans), arrived at much the same conclusion. In relation to older children (i.e., those having reached statutory school-leaving age), Craft and Craft (1983) again found that social class variables could not account for the differences in attainment between Afro-Caribbean, South Asian and white pupils, but their study, too, contained only a small number of Afro-Caribbeans.

In relation to the research on children whose parents or grand-parents migrated from the Indian subcontinent or East Africa, the chief criticism concerns the over-inclusive nature of the category 'Asian'. For while these children, *on average*, were seen in the School Leavers Survey to be performing as well as their white peers, the average itself obscures marked differences between subgroups. The Swann Committee focused on the Bangladeshis as 'the one Asian subgroup whose school achievement was very low indeed', but concern has also been expressed at the performance of Mirpuri Muslims (Parekh, 1985).

A further warning against any complacency in respect of South Asian children's school attainment has recently been sounded by Krutika Tanna (1985). She maintains that although the school leaving qualifications of Asian pupils are, on the basis of the DES data, better than average, such data are misleading because they fail to take into account the age at which the qualifications were obtained. According to Tanna, South Asians are more likely than their peers from other ethnic groups to stay on at school until their late teens. Comparing like with like (i.e., looking at the examination results of all three groups of children at the same age), may show the attainment levels of South Asians in a rather less favourable light.

Where do we go from here?

Some suggestions for improving the quality and usefulness of research in this area have already been intimated. We have implied, for example, that all studies from now on should ensure that they control for both social class and age variables. In addition, we would urge that future research makes use of far larger samples. This would not only allow us to make more meaningful comparisons between distinctive subgroups *within* the South Asian community (and to compare these subgroups with other sections of the population), but would also allow us to extrapolate with more confidence by reducing the sampling error. In other words, it would provide us with more accurate information as to how each group as a whole was faring. We need more substantial data not only to make meaningful comparisons between distinctive South Asian subgroups, but to enable us to do likewise with the different categories of children included under the umbrella terms 'West Indian' and 'All Other Leavers'. The latter, in fact, is an ethnic potpourri comprising children described as African, African or West Indian, All other descriptions and Not recorded. To aggregate such apparently diverse backgrounds into a single category is not only devoid of logic but may blur important distinctions. (In the ILEA Literacy Survey, for example, the attainment levels of Turkish Cypriots were lower than those of Afro-Caribbeans.) The eclectic nature of the category also makes us wonder about the fate of so-called 'mixed race' children. As Anne Wilson (1981, p. 36) has pointed out:

> mixed race children in Britain have received very little socio-logical attention. Recognition of their existence has...been mostly restricted to short paragraphs – references 'en passant' – in works devoted to the wider study of the new ethnic minorities and their relations with the white community.

In the entire literature on ethnic differences in attainment we have yet to come across any reference (*en passant* or otherwise) to the academic attainment of 'mixed race' children. The omission is important not least for methodological reasons. In relation to the extant literature, we wonder how such children have been viewed in the past in terms of the threefold categorization of 'Asian', 'West Indian' and 'Others'. In the Swann Report were they automatically included in 'All other descriptions'? Were some placed in that category and the rest seen as 'West Indians' or 'Asians'? Who decided and on what basis? Bearing in mind the unique problems that often confront such children, can a case be made for examining their educational performance separately, or would such a move simply result in a resurgence of 'scientific racism'? (See Rose, 1979; Barker, 1981.) Whatever the answer to these questions, it would be useful, in future, to at least know how 'mixed-race' children have been treated in the research design.

We also believe that to view Afro-Caribbeans as an undifferentiated entity may be to mask significant differences between subgroups. For as Monica Taylor (1981) notes, there is a consistent suggestion in the literature (e.g., Bagley *et al.*, 1978) that children of Jamaican origin achieve less well than children from other Caribbean islands. (However, we need to exercise caution in interpreting this finding as much of the research into Afro-Caribbean achievement has been undertaken with 'Jamaican' children in the London area where levels of attainment of *all* pupils tend to be lower than in other conurbations. Furthermore, many of the studies reviewed are somewhat dated and thus while island of origin *might* retain some relevance as an explanatory variable, it is probably now of less significance than either social class or gender.)

Although the importance of social class is disputed, the tendency for Afro-Caribbean girls to obtain better results at school than Afro-Caribbean boys (both in Britain and in the West Indies) has been known for some time (e.g., Driver, 1980). We therefore urge that greater attention be paid to gender in researching ethnic differences in attainment. In making this recommendation we are aware that while such differences have also been commented upon frequently in relation to 'all-white' samples, there seems to be relatively little data on gender differences among South Asians. It would be of theoretical interest as well as perhaps of practical value to have such data.

In summing up her very comprehensive review of the literature on Afro-Caribbean attainment, Monica Taylor (1981) makes a number of recommendations for future research. Among other things, she argues for greater variety:

[Few] studies gave sufficiently detailed information on or adequately sampled different types of school, such as single sex, mixed secondary modern or comprehensive, and studies often failed to differentiate between those with small or large numbers of pupils or high and low percentages of ethnic minority pupils on the school rolls.

(Taylor, 1981, p. 213)

She also argues for more longitudinal research, noting that 'very few studies have been able to compare both performance at junior and secondary school age directly'. Although we obviously would not demur at this suggestion, we believe it to be especially important to monitor the progress of Afro-Caribbean children at the infant or first school stage. The basis of our recommendation is research (e.g., Scarr *et al.*, 1983) showing that while such children perform as well as other groups when they start school at the age of five, they begin to fall behind within a couple of years or so. In discussing the educational implications of her own very recent study, Florisse Kysel (1988, p. 89) also argues that:

in order to raise the examination achievement of those ethnic groups who are not doing well, it is necessary to look to primary as well as secondary schools, since these groups were already showing signs of low attainment at the beginning of junior school.

If prevention is better than cure, the early rather than the later stages of schooling ought to become the *chief* focus of concern.

Our final suggestion, however, relates to individual schools at every level. The Swann Report expressed regret that it was unable to proceed with a research proposal to investigate the factors associated with successful Afro-Caribbean pupils. The opposition came from sections of the Afro-Caribbean community itself which understandably felt that the responsibility for underachievement was being laid at its own door rather than where it properly belonged; namely, within the school. While we would not presume to judge the extent to which this opposition was justified, we have to recognize (following Rutter *et al.*, 1979), that schools with very similar catchments may vary markedly in their success rates. We therefore urge researchers to compare *schools* that are similar in their social class and ethnic composition in order to identify and examine more closely those processes thought to act as a restraint upon Afro-Caribbean attainment.

One such process which has not only attracted attention but excited considerable controversy is teacher expectation. We turn now to explore the contours of this debate.

Teacher expectation and Afro-Caribbean attainment

The Rampton Report (1981) acknowledged the many and diverse reasons for what it considered the failure of Afro-Caribbean children to compete academically with children from other ethnic groups. The discovery of an explanatory labyrinth did not, however, inhibit members of Rampton's Committee from attributing the apparently low attainment, in large measure, to a form of racism that it believed was endemic in the teaching profession. Specifically, it accused many teachers of adopting uncritically negative stereotypes of Afro-Caribbean children. The Report (p. 12) stated that:

> a well-intentioned and apparently sympathetic person may, as a result of his [sic] education, experiences or environment, have negative, patronising or stereotyped views about ethnic minority groups.

Teachers falling within this category were regarded by the Committee as guilty of 'unintentional racism', a concept illustrated in the Report (p. 13) by reference to the:

> fairly widespread opinion among teachers... that West Indian pupils inevitably caused difficulties [and were] unlikely to achieve in academic terms.

It further stated that many teachers 'may have high expectations of [West Indians] in areas such as sport, dance drama and art' (p. 13).

The theoretical roots of Rampton's concern with unintentional racism lie in Robert Merton's (1949) seminal discussion of the self-fulfilling prophecy. In *Social Theory and Social Structure* he wrote:

> In the beginning, the self-fulfilling prophecy is a false definition of the situation evolving a new behaviour which makes the originally false conception come 'true'. This specious validity of the self-fulfilling prophecy perpetuates a reign of error. For the

prophet will cite the actual course of events as proof that he was right from the very beginning.

(Merton, 1949, p. 181)

The most celebrated study of the self-fulfilling prophecy in an educational context was undertaken by Rosenthal and Jacobson (1968). Working in a Californian elementary school, they 'informed' a group of teachers (on the basis of a spurious IQ test) that some pupils in each class would make considerably more progress than others over the coming year. Rosenthal and Jacobson not only claim to have demonstrated the truth of their prediction, but argue that it materialized because the teachers acted in accordance with their induced expectations.

In view of its implications, it is not surprising that this study received considerable publicity in academic circles. Much of it, though, has been critical. Among other things, it has been pointed out that there were only two classes in the entire school where there was any significant difference between children who were nominated as 'bloomers' and those who were not. There were no expectancy effects in grades three to six and in one class the experimental hypothesis not only failed to materialize, but was actually reversed! Moreover, the IQ scores ranged from zero to 300 leading Mackintosh and Mascie-Taylor to conclude that the test was either absurd or administered quite inappropriately.

Similar attempts to demonstrate the importance of induced teacher expectations have generally been unsuccessful. In contrast, the influence of *naturalistic* expectations on teachers' behaviour (e.g., Palardy, 1969) is empirically well-established and provides the justification for the Rampton Report embracing the self-fulfilling prophecy as an explanatory construct and according it a pivotal role in explaining ethnic differences in attainment. But, as Brophy and Good (1970) and more recently, Derek Blease (1983) have argued, the causal link between teachers' expectations and their pupils' performance is not automatic. Brophy and Good assert that initially teachers have to believe that certain standards of behaviour and levels of achievement are characteristic of specific pupils. If they then act towards these pupils in accordance with their beliefs, a self-fulfilling prophecy will ensue. However, the effects will only have a lasting impact if the pupils change their self-concept as a result of correctly interpreting and then internalizing their teachers' perceptions.

Brophy and Good argue that if teachers behave consistently over time, and pupils accept the validity of their evaluations, then the behaviour and achievement of pupils will increasingly conform to their teachers' original expectations.

The first stage of this model thus requires that we examine the claim that negative stereotyping of Afro-Caribbean children is (or has been) widespread within the teaching profession. A number of studies beginning with Elaine Brittan's (1976) survey of both primary and secondary teachers offers at least prima facie support for the allegation. Corroboration can be found in the work of Michael Rutter et al. (1974), Sally Tomlinson (1979), and Bruce Carrington and Edward Wood (1983). These studies are fully compatible with Rampton's claim that, not infrequently, teachers enter the classroom armed with stereotypes that threaten the academic success of their Afro-Caribbean pupils. But the studies are equally compatible with an alternative and contrary hypothesis; namely, that teachers are not wedded to any particular belief about Afro-Caribbean children prior to encountering them and form their attitudes solely on the basis of subsequent interaction. Thus, the negative attitudes sampled in the research cited above may reflect a classroom reality rather than create one.

The Rampton Report did not consider the possibility of Afro-Caribbean children influencing the expectations of their teachers. Instead, it promoted the idea of racial stereotyping as an aspect of socialization to which many potential teachers fall victim, only later to initiate the chain of events that culminate in 'underachievement'. Such an argument, however, is unconvincing as there are no a priori grounds for assuming that a high proportion of teachers will accept rather than reject the racist aspects of their upbringing. While all occupational groups may be equally exposed to the forces of prejudice, it should not be assumed that they are all equally open to persuasion. In addition to this theoretical weakness, Rampton's emphasis on the role of teacher socialization is empirically suspect. There is no evidence, in the Report or elsewhere, of the extent to which teachers acquire beliefs about Afro-Caribbean children before meeting them, and more seriously, the Report fails to acknowledge the literature that does exist on the way that pupils can shape their teachers' expectations and thus their behaviour. In relation to gender, for example, Jane French (1986) has recently reported a study of infant classrooms in which:

the girls were, in comparative terms, model pupils. Although interested and eager to participate; they tended to comply with the classroom rules ... Their very observance of these rules made them unproblematic from the point of view of class discipline and, consequently, meant that the teacher devoted less time to them.

So, although the teachers *may* have held sexist attitudes which influenced the ways in which they treated their pupils, the behaviour of the pupils also exerted an influence. (Original emphasis.)

(French, 1986, p. 404)

With specific reference to race, the pupil's role in moulding teacher expectation has been explored by Short (1983). In this study it was found that teachers tended to describe children on the basis of their individual personalities rather than the stereotype commonly associated with their racial identity. For example, while 'West Indian' girls were perceived as poorly behaved in comparison with their 'white' and 'Asian' counterparts, the same was not the case for 'West Indian' boys. This sex difference has no parallel in the cultural stereotype. Findings such as these indicate that while teachers may, at some point, subscribe to culturally induced expectations of Afro-Caribbean children, such expectations are modified in the light of contrary evidence derived from personal contact. Teachers' expectations ought thus to be viewed not as inflexible by-products of socialization, but rather as fluid constructs that can accommodate individual differences. Joseph Guttmann (1984) supports this contention. On the basis of research carried out in Israel, he concluded that:

When people are asked to judge others on the basis of information irrelevant to the matter of judgement, they rely on their stereotypic perception. When, however, they are provided with closely relevant information ... they tend to accord that information overriding importance and give up their stereotypic perception.

(Guttmann, 1984, p. 10)

The studies by Short and Guttmann suggest that even if teachers accept a racial or ethnic stereotype in principle, they will acknowledge its partial or complete irrelevance for particular children belonging to the group concerned. Thus a teacher's behaviour towards an Afro-Caribbean child may bear little resemblance to the same teacher's attitude towards Afro-Caribbean people as a whole. This possibility is strengthened by well-known studies in social psychology (e.g., LaPiere, 1934) showing a lack of correspondence, under certain circumstances, between measured attitudes and observed behaviour. Research by Weigel *et al.* (1974) indicates that the disjunction between attitude and behaviour is likely to be especially marked when the former relates to a broad issue and the latter to a specific instance (e.g., attitudes towards Afro-Caribbean children in general and behaviour towards an individual Afro-Caribbean child).

While it is likely that many teachers behave towards Afro-Caribbean pupils in ways that are consistent with prevailing stereotypes, there is no evidence to support Rampton's allegation that they behave in ways *determined* by such stereotypes. Even if we assume that teachers do pre-judge their Afro-Caribbean pupils, the means by which they communicate their expectations offers scant support to Rampton. For research (Good, 1980) shows that not all teachers who share the same belief about a group of children will respond to them in the same manner. The research distinguishes between 'overreactive' and 'proactive' teachers. The former characteristically exaggerate the intellectual differences between children and supply quantitatively and qualitatively better treatment to the high achieving. The latter, in contrast, actually give less able children more time and attention than their numbers warrant, but they attempt to do so without disadvantaging the rest of the class. A third group of teachers occupy an intermediate position and are described as 'reactive'. They allow the academically talented to come to the fore but without offering them undue encouragement.

Studies of white teachers in multiracial schools (e.g., Leacock, 1971; Rubovits and Maehr, 1973) have tended to focus less upon this tripartite division than upon the teachers' feelings towards the children and the details of their interaction. Some have also had a rather tenuous connection with classroom reality. Rubovits and Maehr, for instance, employed undergraduate students in the role of teachers and had them working with groups of just four pupils. While they found evidence of discriminatory behaviour towards the black children, the practical implications of the research are uncertain for two reasons. The first is its artificiality; the second is that the researchers failed to provide any convincing data on their students' racial attitudes. The claim that 'most of [them] expressed liberal beliefs' is hardly compelling.

Perhaps the most important finding to emerge from the study by Rubovits and Maehr, and one which seems to have escaped the notice of most commentators, concerns the danger of generalizing about teachers. This follows from their observation that the tendency for a student to show prejudice towards a black child was positively correlated with the student's level of dogmatism, as measured by the Rokeach Dogmatism Scale (Rokeach, 1960). A much publicised British study drawing attention to the same danger, has recently been conducted by Peter Green (1983). He worked with 70 teachers of children aged between seven and 13 and was particularly interested in how the 12 most ethnocentric teachers in his sample differed from the 12 least ethnocentric in terms of their behaviour towards European, Asian and West Indian children. (The term ethnocentrism, as employed in this study, seems to us, as to members of the Swann Committee, to be little more than a euphemism for individual racism. We discuss the implications of this definition when appraising the value of the study.) Differences were assessed with the aid of a Flanders (1970) schedule. Green observed that teachers, irrespective of their tolerance level for ethnic minorities, accorded roughly the same order of priority to the ten modes of teaching identified in the schedule when dealing with 'West Indian' boys. The intolerant teachers, though, offered these boys less individual teaching time than their numbers warranted and were thus, in Good's terms, 'overreactors'. 'Highly tolerant' teachers, in contrast, were seen to be 'proactive', for they gave Afro-Caribbean boys more than their fair share of individual attention, but in common with their less tolerant colleagues, attached a high priority to criticism and other control strategies. In relation to Afro-Caribbean girls, the differences between highly tolerant and intolerant teachers were even more marked, for they were found in connection with both the order of priority given to the ten categories and in the frequency with which the categories were used.

This study is important for several reasons. In the first instance, it casts a shadow of doubt over the claim that teachers who are sympathetic to Afro-Caribbean children are none the less likely to teach them in ways influenced by the racial stereotype. 'Highly tolerant' teachers, for example, gave both Afro-Caribbean boys and girls, a disproportionate amount of praise and encouragement. Secondly, by revealing that 'highly tolerant' teachers respond less favourably to Afro-Caribbean boys than girls (in terms of the order of priority accorded the various categories) it reinforces the argument made earlier, that teachers' behaviour may be determined, in part, by the behaviour of their pupils. The apparent concern of both 'tolerant' and 'intolerant' teachers to control the behaviour of Afro-Caribbean boys also supports this conclusion. Thirdly, the study is of value because of Green's view of ethnocentrism as a 'tendency to consider the characteristics and attitudes of ethnic groups other than one's own to be inferior' (p. 102). This definition suggests that the highly ethnocentric teachers in the study overlap to a considerable degree with those who are explicitly racist. As the latter, according to Rampton, are comparatively rare, and the former, according to Green, the most likely to show discriminatory behaviour, Rampton's belief in the widespread effects of unintentional racism would seem exaggerated.

The legitimacy of Rampton's concern with Afro-Caribbean children's self-concept rests on two assumptions. The first is that such children not only have a relatively poor self-concept but one that suffers from the actions of unintentionally racist teachers. The second is that the self-concept is causally related to scholastic achievement. Both are contentious. In relation to the former, Blease (1983) argues that one necessary condition for the success of a self-fulfilling prophecy in an educational context is that pupils regard their teachers as significant others. But as Maureen Stone (1981) points out, this condition may not apply as far as many Afro-Caribbean children are concerned:

> In looking critically at the ideas underlying self-concept theory and research... one major contradiction has emerged: given the level of dislike of teachers it is virtually impossible for teachers to be 'significant others' in the lives of West Indian children.
>
> (Stone, 1981, p. 242)

Thus, even if it could be demonstrated that Afro-Caribbean children, as a group, have an inadequate self-concept, we might be wary of attributing responsibility to their teachers. In fact, Green's work, suggests that there is no basis for such a demonstration as he found a clear relationship – indeed a negative correlation – between Afro-Caribbean children's self-concept and their teachers' so called 'ethnocentrism'. Because of the nature of correlation, we cannot be sure that the two phenomena are causally linked, but even assuming this to be the case, we should note that Green's sample comprised only teachers with extreme levels of ethnocentrism. We cannot deduce from this evidence how teachers who are moderately 'ethnocentric', and who may well be in the majority, actually behave towards their Afro-Caribbean pupils. Martin Hammersley (1981, cited in Jeffcoate, 1984) for example, commented on a high degree of staffroom racism (in the form of derogatory remarks) in his ethnographic study of a secondary modern school but found no carry over into the classroom. He wrote: 'the teachers did *not* explicitly discriminate on grounds of race in their dealings with pupils, nor did I detect any covert discrimination, though this of course is much more difficult to identify'.

Some commentators have also expressed reservations about the supposed link between self-concept and academic achievement. Calsyn and Kenny (1977), for example, argue that the latter exerts more of an influence on self-concept than the other way round; a point of view supported by Bridgeman and Shipman (1978). They found that while pre-school children tend to have a uniformly high self-concept, within two or three years of starting school the uniformity has given way to differentiation.

In reviewing the debate over the importance of teacher expectation, we have drawn attention to a number of unresolved issues, both theoretical and empirical. In the light of their complexity, we feel unable to support unequivocally either side of the argument and would advise others to exercise a similar caution before indicting teacher expectation as a major architect of ethnic differences in achievement.

Voluntary and separate schooling

The growth of the voluntary (or supplementary) school movement since the late 1960s has been a direct response to Afro-Caribbean parents' concern at the low attainment levels of their children. According to Chevannes and Reeves (1987, p. 159):

> The existence of the black voluntary school is predicated on the black population's unsatisfactory experience and appraisal of British education – an experience composed of all the classical

ingredients of social alienation: powerlessness, meaninglessness, social isolation and self-estrangement.

In relation to powerlessness, the Afro-Caribbean community has long felt itself unable to influence the nature and direction of mainstream education. The comparatively small number of Afro-Caribbean teachers, and their conspicuous absence from positions of authority, the limited representation of Afro-Caribbeans on school governing bodies and on LEA committees are all likely to have contributed to this feeling of impotence. Compounding these parental frustrations, Chevannes and Reeves assert that 'black pupils struggle to gain greater mastery of their immediate situation by developing collective strategies which often run counter to the aims of the school and are possibly injurious to their own career prospects' (1987, p. 159).

There are two reasons for thinking that black pupils in mainstream schools may suffer a sense of meaninglessness. The first is that the curriculum often fails to reflect their interests, experiences and culture. In contrast, the study of black people's struggle to survive and achieve in the face of adversity, generally assumes a significant role in the curriculum of voluntary schools. Chevannes and Reeves believe that older black pupils in particular are prone to experience a feeling of meaninglessness for another reason; namely, their more instrumental approach to education. In making this assertion, they would appear to share Maureen Stone's (1981) view that the 'basic enabling skills' which feature so prominently in the voluntary school movement, are treated with insufficient seriousness in black children's full-time day schools. But in fairness to the latter, it should be pointed out that voluntary schools do not seem to be totally successful in attracting and retaining the interest of older children. In her discussion of Saturday schools, Stone (1981, pp. 185-6) noted that 'it was always the boys who dropped out first, usually when they were about thirteen or fourteen, whereas the girls kept on until sometimes after sixteen' (cf. Driver, 1980).

As far as isolation is concerned, the argument in favour of voluntary schools is that black children are bound to feel more secure where black people are not only in the majority but are seen to be in control. Black teachers, too, are likely to feel more comfortable and operate more effectively in an environment where they do not have to confront the ostracism of some white colleagues and the overt prejudice of some white children. However, the voluntary school as a solution to social isolation may parodoxically reduce still further the contact between black and white people.

The fourth and final element of social alienation as described by Chevannes and Reeves is self-estrangement. In relation to the black experience in Britain, this refers to the black child's sense of self. Although Maureen Stone, among others, refers to research showing that black children now possess a level of self-esteem equal to that of other 'racial' groups, the self-image of the black child has remained one of the prime concerns of the black voluntary school movement. Thus not only is a concerted effort made to expunge ethnocentric materials from the curriculum in such schools, but black teachers in prominent positions are encouraged and valued as professional role models.

While it may be useful to assess the voluntary school movement in terms of its academic, social and emotional benefits to black children, it would seem rather more important to examine the response of the educational establishment to those anxieties of black parents which led to the establishment of the schools in the first nstance.

In some respects there seems to have been little improvement. For example, we referred in Chapter 5 to the Commission for Racial Equality's recent survey showing how few black teachers there are in maintained schools, even in ethnically mixed areas. Yet in other respects, such as the increased number of LEAs and individual schools formally committed to antiracist and multicultural policies, it appears that the education system has undergone significant change. However, some commentators, notably Troyna and Ball (1985), have questioned the commitment underlying the rhetoric of such policy statements, and the Swann Report also takes a less optimistic view of these and other recent developments. Commenting on separate, rather than supplementary black schools, it notes:

> Some West Indian parents groups and certain leading West Indian educationalists have continued to believe that the only way in which West Indian children can hope to succeed in educational terms is through attending separate 'Black' schools since they regard existing schools as irremediably racist and dismiss any moves towards developing multicultural education as merely

cosmetic and as in no way tackling the fundamental inequalities and injustices inherent in the system.

(Swann Report, 1985, p. 515)

The Swann Committee argued that the demand for separate, and presumably supplementary, black schools would evaporate if the recommendations in its report were acted upon. The majority of the Committee felt the same way about demands from the Asian community for its own separate schools, an issue we now consider.

For a number of cultural and religious reasons, various ethnic minority groups have for some time sought to establish their own separate voluntary-aided schools as an alternative to existing main-stream provision. Their rights in this respect are firmly enshrined in law and are thus no different from those enjoyed by other denomina-tions whether Anglican, Catholic or Jewish. (Despite this equality before the law, Mohamed Naguib (1986) points out that Swann insists on referring to the proposed schools as 'separate' rather than as denominational, thereby suggesting a demand beyond the law. 'It conjures up images and reinforces views that 'they do not want to integrate, that they do not wish to be part of society' (p. 8).)

South Asian parents who support separate schools, tend to believe that their children's religious traditions are more likely to flourish if taught by committed adherents in an environment free from what they regard as the antagonistic influences of either the Christian-dominated or secular ethos of mainstream schools. Discussing the particular dilemmas faced by the Muslim community, Halstead and Khan-Cheema (1987, p. 24) suggest that during the course of the 1980s 'many Muslims have become increasingly dissatisfied with the position in which they have found themselves in relation to religious education and school worship'. Their unease hinges upon three major issues. The first concerns the legal right of withdrawal from religious worship, a right they are happy to retain but would rather not exercise. Their preference would be 'to see modifications in the form taken by religious education and school assemblies so that Muslims could take part without compromising their faith' (1987, p. 24). The second problem relates to a teaching approach based on world religions. Misgivings here arise over teaching focusing on 'interesting social or cultural features of world faiths to the exclusion of any teaching of general religious, spiritual or moral principles' (1987, p. 25). Finally, Halstead and Khan-Cheema refer to fears about the secularization of religious education as epitomized by Afzal Rahman (1977), former chairman of the Muslim Educational Trust:

> There seems to be a general trend among all opinions, including religious as well as secular, towards more liberalism in religious education leading almost to a non-religious or an irreligious type of religious education in schools... This type of education is diametrically opposed to the Islamic philosophy of education.

In common with moves by the Afro-Caribbean community to support the establishment of both separate and supplementary schools, South Asian groups have also expressed unease at the Anglocentric nature of the curriculum which they believe still predominates in many schools. They not only resent the neglect of Asian history and literature as well as other aspects of their culture, but feel strongly that insufficient support and encouragement is given to the teaching of community languages. (The difficulty of reconciling these educational concerns, and those of other ethnic groups, with the maintainance of social cohesion, presents policy makers with what Brian Bullivant (1981) refers to as 'the pluralist dilemma'. From time to time, parents too, appear to have difficulty in coming to terms with an educational system that aims to celebrate both diversity and unity; witness the Honeyford affair (Foster-Carter, 1987) and recent developments at Dewsbury.)

Not the least important of the reasons advanced by some sections of the South Asian community for setting up its own schools is the insulation they could provide from various manifestations of racism. The 'playground' murder in September 1986 of Ahmed Iqbal Ullah, a Manchester 13-year-old, may be thought to provide a particularly poignant illustration of the need for such insulation. Rather less dramatically, the Swann Report also points out that some South Asian teachers see themselves as the victims of racism in terms of their employment and promotion prospects. They view the creation of Sikh and Muslim schools as a means of widening their opportunities for career advancement.

Among the various South Asian pressure groups calling for separate schools, it is the demand for single-sex education made by *some* members of the Muslim community which, in recent years, has most sharply divided informed opinion. The issue at the heart of the debate concerns the education of Muslim girls and in particular, the appropriateness of the curriculum. This is not simply a question of the prohibitions on joint participation with boys in sex education and in swimming and other forms of physical education that we alluded to in Chapter 5, but a more fundamental conflict over the type of provision thought suitable for Muslim girls. On the basis of statements 'made by spokesmen of the Muslim community', the Swann Report (1985, p. 505) claimed:

> it is clear that the form of single sex education which at least some of them are advocating for girls would entail a far more central focus in the curriculum on education for marriage and mother-hood in a particular Islamic sense, with other subjects receiving less attention and with the notion of careers education being seen as irrelevant to the pattern of adult life which the girls were likely to pursue.

According to Philip Walkling and Chris Brannigan (1986), the prospect of separate schools for Muslim girls operating on the basis of these guidelines presents a possible dilemma for the liberal-minded educationalist who is also committed to anti-sexism. They argue that the dilemma arises:

> only when we forget who our clients are and, out of a misguided sense of tolerance forget that the ultimate bearers of educational rights are individual children and not their parents or their parents' representatives.
>
> If you regard the emancipation and equalization of women as a primary objective of society and its education system, then your decisions with regard to equal opportunities (gender) would follow from this. If some groups of people wish to protect 'their women' to some degree by having separate schools then this should be resisted.

Walkling and Brannigan go on to challenge those such as Naguib (1985) who defend the creation of separate Muslim schools partly on the grounds that other religious denominations have exercised their legal rights in this respect. They assert that all such schools are divisive and should be absorbed into the state system.

However, the dilemma that Walkling and Brannigan envisage between antiracist and antisexist education has been dismissed by

Troyna and Carrington (1987). They maintain that 'a pluralist approach in education *does not entail* that everything and anything goes', and accuse Walkling and Brannigan of misconstruing the tenor and thrust of both cultural pluralism and antiracism by suggesting otherwise. Troyna and Carrington also dispute the claim that most educational provision for girls within Muslim schools would necessarily conflict with antisexist demands. Citing the work of Rosemary Deem (1984) and Judith Whyte (1986), they argue that 'some types of single sex provision... could be conducive to the realization of antisexist goals'.

Apparently unaware of this possibility, the majority of the Swann Committee expressed the same reservations as Walking and Brannigan concerning the compatibility of the formal curriculum of Muslim schools with antisexist principles and practices. They also opposed the setting up of such schools for a number of other reasons. To begin with, they felt that the anxieties expressed by some Muslim parents would be much diminished if the recommendations of their Report were implemented. They claimed, too, that separation might not only exacerbate feelings of rejection but extend the scope for 'inter-racial' misunderstanding, not least by failing to remedy 'the inaccurate and misleading stereotypes of ethnic minority groups which persist in the minds of the majority'.

At the same time, however, the Committee felt that existing schools could do more 'to respond to the "pastoral" needs of Muslim pupils so that Muslim parents are no longer seen as simply "being awkward"'. There are, of course, long established precedents for maintained schools in this country accommodating the religious obligations and proscriptions of minority groups. Michael Dickenson (1988), for example, in describing the immigrant Jewish community in Leeds at the turn of the century, tells us:

In other ways the Leylands School (both infant and junior) tried to accommodate its timetable to the needs of a multicultural approach. This took several forms. For example, by the later 1890s, the various Jewish religious festivals had become official school holidays, such that on 15 September 1899, the infants department closed for the full eight days of the Feast of Tabernacles, and such practices were also true of the junior department. To take another example, both Infants and Junior Departments finished school at 3 p.m. on Friday afternoon in winter to allow the children time to reach home before the Sabbath. It can, of course, be argued that, with such a large Jewish population, such policy decisions were the only practical alternative to large-scale disruption of lessons caused by absenteeism. No doubt this is true, but such policy decisions also seem to have been deliberate, a gesture of good faith to the Jewish community. Previously, in the early 1890s the school had remained open for the Jewish festivals, and one feels that the change of policy was to some extent aimed at receiving the support of the local people.

(Dickenson, 1988, p. 43)

The Swann Report urged existing schools to take further steps towards meeting the cultural needs of Muslim girls by expanding single-sex provision across the curriculum to include field trips and organized school holidays. However, the Committee recognized that such changes could go only so far in meeting the concerns of those parents who desire single-sex schools for their daughters. They therefore recommended that LEAs retain or re-establish the option of single-sex education.

The minority view among the Swann Committee (p. 515) was that while the realization of *Education for All* might indeed render separate schools superfluous, 'an emphasis on an ideal future may be an excuse for inaction in the present and for failure to meet immediate needs'. They did not, though, dissent from the majority view that

> if teachers showed themselves willing to cooperate in a positive way with community-based activities and to respond sensitively to pastoral concerns and to take effective action to tackle all manifestations of racism, whether overt or covert... much of the mistrust and frustration which lies behind arguments for an alternative to existing schools would be overcome.
>
> (Swann Report, 1985, p. 509)

The implications for teacher education are self-evident.

7
Teacher Education and the Prospects for Change

Criticisms have long been made about the failure of both initial (IT) and in-service (INSET) teacher education to meet the professional needs of teachers in a multiracial and multicultural society. Despite repeated censure by various independent and official bodies throughout the 1970s, the available evidence suggests that few institutions had begun any systematic review of this provision by 1981 (e.g., Rampton Report, 1981). Whereas we recognize that steps have subsequently been taken to overcome this institutional inertia, we are not sanguine about the continuing prospects for reform. The measures are being introduced at a time when the whole of teacher education is in disarray, as a result of financial constraints, the pressures imposed by accreditation at IT level and changed funding arrangements at INSET level, and uncertainty surrounding the implementation of the National Curriculum.

We begin this chapter by assessing the response of teacher education to 'race' and ethnicity and consider, in passing, major initiatives in the area. On the basis of this appraisal and our foregoing analysis, we make a number of policy recommendations. Among other things, the potential of access courses, as a means of increasing the recruitment of ethnic minorities to teaching, is underlined. While we recognize that it is important for teachers to reflect upon their own and others' taken-for-granted assumptions about 'race', we argue that Racism Awareness Training programmes, in their present form, do not provide an appropriate vehicle for changing attitudes and behaviour. In view of the reluctance of many primary teachers to discuss racism and other controversial issues with their pupils and the tendency for staff in this sector to perceive such issues as largely beyond the grasp of younger children, we urge that more attention is given at both IT and INSET level to the following: the development of forms of collective identity and awareness, including 'race'; political and moral socialization; age-related and spatial variations in children's understanding of topics relating to power, social justice and human rights; and strategies for handling contentious subject matter in the classroom. To allay practitioners' unease about aspects of antiracist and multicultural education and facilitate the development of a positive and reflective approach to curriculum innovation in this sphere, we emphasize the importance of school-focused INSET with whole staffs. In addition, we stress the need for teachers to engage in small-scale action research to monitor and evaluate such initiatives. From the standpoint that the *process* of teaching and learning is no less important than curriculum *content*, especially in courses dealing with social justice and human rights, we consider the view that teacher educators need to reappraise their own pedagogy and move from 'a lecturing mode towards a transactional model which recognizes and utilizes the experience and expertise of the participants' (Burtonwood, 1986, p. 33).

Pressures for reform

In 1981, a seemingly exasperated House of Commons Select Committee on Racial Disadvantage made the following observation about the failure of teacher education to adopt a pluralist perspective:

> The issues involved have now been kicked around interested parties for so many years that it is no longer acceptable to wait for the complex administrative structure of teacher training to come to terms in its own good time with the challenge presented by the multiracial classroom. It is against a background of justified weariness and impatience that we must consider how teacher training must now tardily adapt to this challenge.
>
> (House of Commons, 1981, p. 59)

Teacher education was also attacked in other major reports published that year. The Rampton Committee, for example, noted that the evidence it had received 'presented an overwhelming picture of the failure of teacher training institutions to prepare teachers for their role in a multiracial society' (Rampton Report, 1981, p. 60). This depressing appraisal was also supported by the findings of a national survey of IT provision (Giles and Cherrington, 1981), and by an evaluation of INSET provision in multicultural education (Eggleston, Dunn and Purewal, 1981).

Giles and Cherrington found that, whereas two-thirds of polytechnic and half of college IT courses made reference to 'race' and ethnicity, only a third of universities did so. Much of this provision was optional and 'focused almost exclusively on the background and heritage of black groups to the exclusion of all others'. In their view, 'this emphasis on cultural differences, however well-intentioned, resulted in black groups being perceived in isolation from the dominant white society' (1981, pp. 81–2). In the light of this evidence, it is not surprising to find that the Inspectorate, in a national survey of probationer teachers, were to report in the following year that less than half of those approached felt that they had been 'adequately prepared to teach children from different cultural backgrounds' (DES, 1982).

A similarly bleak picture of INSET provision at this juncture is provided by the DES-funded Keele survey, *Inservice Teacher Education in a Multiracial Society* (Eggleston *et al.* 1981, p.91). Commenting on its findings, the project director, John Eggleston (1981, p. 91) has noted:

Our investigations have left us in no doubt about the fragmentary and incomplete provision of inservice teacher education for a multicultural society. Indeed, it is non-existent in many areas and in none is it wholly adequate.

The survey suggested that the *potential* demand for INSET courses may not have been fully realized, even though the 'sluggish' demand for some courses had led to their cancellation. Some staff had failed to secure release from their schools to attend day-time courses because this type of INSET experience was not generally accorded 'proper recognition' in appointment and promotion procedures. The importance of school-based curriculum development, in overcoming staff resistance to these (and other) innovations, was emphasized by Eggleston, who argued (p. 58) that INSET:

must be school-oriented, directed to the needs and practices of participants and their institutions. It is important that this is not directed in a prescriptive way, but rather in a manner that encourages participants themselves to innovate and build upon the experiences of their schools and the course.

Acknowledging the difficulties associated with any form of course evaluation, he none the less claimed that it was possible to discern 'a noticeable shift' from 'assimilatory to cultural pluralist goals' among his respondents. There was little evidence, however, of any discernible move towards what would now be described as antiracism. According to Eggleston (p. 101):

> A particular characteristic of teachers who had attended the short courses seemed to be a willingness to settle for somewhat better 'survival skills' rather than to be more determined and better equipped to tackle the major issues of prejudice, differential opportunity and the like.

The indictment of teacher education continued with the publication of the Swann Report (1985) which castigated the 'paucity of provision' and 'lack of progress' in relation to the 'multicultural aspects' of IT, and reiterated (in the absence of up-to-date information) Eggleston's criticisms of INSET. Although the Swann Committee may have been correct in its appraisal, there were signs that some positive changes had already begun. For example, the Council for National Academic Awards (CNAA) discussion paper, 'Multicultural Education', which was first circulated to 'public sector' teacher education institutions in July 1984, can be regarded as a major step forward. The paper set out to suggest 'the aims and objectives of multicultural and antiracist education in a teacher education con.ext', and to raise issues which 'are relevant across the spectrum of teacher education, whatever the age phase or subject-specialism of the teacher'. Focusing on course content and provision, it called upon teacher education institutions to take account of the following when devising 'permeation strategies', or producing 'core-course elements' and 'special options'.

> Teachers need to (i) be equipped to prepare all young people for life in a multicultural and racially harmonious society; (ii) have an awareness and understanding of racism both historically and in

contemporary society and to be conscious of the various forms in which racism can manifest itself; (iii) have an awareness of intercultural relations and their social and economic contexts; (iv) be able to teach with skill and sensitivity in schools and further education institutions recognising any particular needs of ethnic minority pupils and students; (v) interact effectively with colleagues in an institutional framework in relation to these issues.

(CNAA, 1984, p. 2)

Although recognizing that the needs of prospective teachers and experienced teachers can be different, the discussion paper recommended that IT and INSET courses, *inter alia*, should equip practitioners: to adopt a 'critical approach to cultural bias, prejudice, racism and stereotyping' in teaching schemes, texts and other materials; to recognize 'the value of teaching which acknowledges the aspirations of all pupils and students, and which seeks to enhance their chances of realising these aspirations'; to be 'sensitive to the presence of unintentional racism in their own expectations, evaluations of and attitudes towards students from ethnic minority groups'; to deal appropriately with incidents of overt racism; and to regard 'cultural diversity as a source of social and curriculum enrichment'. In addition, the document invited institutions to consider their staffing and staff development policies, and to establish a coordinator and committee to develop and implement a policy on multicultural and antiracist education. However, no real guidance was given to indicate *how* this process of institutional change might be effected.

These guidelines were later incorporated (in a slightly revised form) in a parallel document produced by the Universities Council for the Education of Teachers (UCET, February 1986). They remained in use throughout the 'public sector' until December 1986, when another policy statement was issued by the CNAA. As a result of political pressure, however, the CNAA retreated from 'its clear espousal of antiracism' (Menter, 1988). In its new guidelines, all references to antiracist education were expunged and replaced with the seemingly innocuous (but nebulous) phrase: 'education provided without racial discrimination'.

Many of the recommendations made by the CNAA about course content and provision in its 1984 policy document were echoed by the Swann Committee the following year. In contrast to the CNAA, the Committee outlined in detail the various organizational strategies needed to surmount institutional inertia in teacher education. It is to these proposals that we now turn.

At IT level, Swann argued that the racial attitudes of student teachers should be monitored:

> We believe that if a student demonstrates, by his actions or behaviour during taught studies or teaching practice, deep-seated and openly racist views about ethnic minority groups which materially affect the way he teaches and which do not appear to be open to reason or change through training, that should be an important element in assessing whether he or she is temperamentally suitable to enter the teaching profession.
>
> (Swann Report, 1985, p. 569)

The practical problems associated with such a proposal are, of course, immense, as demonstrated by the judicious evasion of the issue in the report.

To complement core and optional studies dealing with 'race' and ethnicity, Swann and his colleagues urged teacher education institutions to make efforts 'to ensure that all of their students have the opportunity of gaining some practical experience in a multiracial school' (p. 565). IT staff, it was argued, could also benefit from such placements. As well as filling a perceived gap in the experience of some lecturers (by permitting, for example, closer links with practising teachers), such links could help ensure that institutions meet the accreditation criterion that a 'sufficient proportion' of staff must have 'recent, substantial and relevant school experience' (DES, 1983a).

The Committee also called upon the Council for the Accreditation of Teacher Education (CATE) to take account of this and related proposals when approving IT courses. Finally, the need to increase ethnic minority participation in IT was underlined.

Recognizing the crucial role of INSET in curriculum innovation and change, Swann recommended that multicultural education should be a national priority area in the in-service education of teachers. In particular, the value of school-based INSET was stressed, because such provision 'is likely to have the most immediate impact on the greatest number of teachers' (Swann Report, 1985, p. 593). As well as calling for courses aimed at senior school staff who could function as 'change agents in their own institutions', the Committee outlined a number of measures to facilitate the implementation of its policies in mainly white areas, including: 'a series of pilot projects involving teacher training staff, LEAs and schools... designed to develop and disseminate good practice in this field' (p. 590). Aware of the controversy surrounding Racism Awareness Training Programmes, the Committee asked the DES to fund an 'independent evaluation of their content and effectiveness.'

To assess the responses of teacher education to these various pressures for reform, we now consider the extant research since 1985.

Antiracism, multiculturalism and initial teacher education

In contrast to the Swann Committee's bleak appraisal, a number of recent studies of antiracist and multicultural education provision in initial teacher education have presented a slightly more sanguine view of developments in this sphere. In 1985, for example, Andy Hannan published the findings of a study evaluating the impact of Birmingham Polytechnic's BEd course on a sample of 167 first, second and third year students. The investigation was carried out in 1982/3; the orientation of the course at this juncture was described as: 'expressly committed to educating all its students to teach in a multicultural society', but as far from taking a committed antiracist stance. On the basis of a questionnaire survey, supplemented by 13 in-depth interviews, he reported:

a surprising degree of acceptance on the students' part of the multiculturalist philosophy, some worrying evidence from a minority of students of a failure to counter racist assumptions and a lack of penetration of multicultural, let alone antiracist issues in important parts of the course.

(Hannan, 1985, p. 21)

These findings were broadly corroborated by a similar evaluation undertaken at the College of St Paul and St Mary in Cheltenham, during the academic year 1985/6 (Menter, 1987). As a result of mounting staff and student dissatisfaction with a 'permeation approach' to antiracist and multicultural education, a conference style programme (of three and a half days duration which addressed the topic of 'Racism and Education') had been incorporated in the second year of the primary BEd course. Employing a modified version of Hannan's questionnaire, Menter undertook a quasi-experiment in an attempt to find out whether the programme had resulted in any discernible change in the students' attitudes to antiracist or multicultural education. (The evaluation was based on the assumption that the two perspectives are mutually exclusive.) Menter found that there was 'overall support for multicultural initiatives' and this support increased substantially during the programme. In contrast, attitudes towards antiracism (which, at the outset, were fairly positive) remained largely unchanged throughout the initiative. Although the feedback from the students was described as 'typically positive', many had made 'a strong plea for participation from black speakers in order "to get a wider perspective"' (Menter, 1987, p. 41).

A questionnaire survey undertaken in 1983 by the present authors (Carrington, Millward and Short, 1986) not only revealed similar attitudes to current educational policies on 'race', but also highlighted some of the shortcomings of initial teacher education courses in this area. The study, which sought to make a direct comparison between primary and secondary students, was based on a sample of 180 students, selected at random from five institutions spread across the north of England and the Midlands and which represented, in all relevant respects, both sides of the binary divide. The student teachers were either taking the PGCE or completing the final year of a BEd. Of those planning to work in primary or middle schools, 14 were male and 66 female; 69 were enrolled on BEd courses and 11 on PGCE. Of the 80 students in the sample intending to teach at secondary level, just over half (43) were female, and just under half (35) were working for the BEd. In percentage terms, these figures broadly reflected the national scene.

The survey indicated that 'whilst the student sample overall adopted a fairly liberal and progressive attitude towards the role of the school in a multiracial society, the trend was more pronounced among primary students' (Carrington, *et al.*, 1986, p. 23). (Following Alexander (1984), we hypothesized that this finding may *in part* be attributable to the differences between primary and secondary teachers, in their occupational identity, role and socialization. We contended that the class teacher system prevalent in primary schools may result in staff perceiving their role in more holistic terms than their secondary counterparts. Regular and protracted contact with the same group of children may ensure that primary teachers accord greater importance to the personal and social development of their pupils. In contrast, the particular demands of specialist teaching, the constraints imposed by external examinations and the frequently formal separation of pedagogical and pastoral roles, may prompt secondary teachers to interpret their relationship, both to pupils and the curriculum, in a more narrowly defined manner.) Our respondents made a number of critical observations about the quality of those aspects of their training which dealt with the role of the school in a multiethnic, multiracial society. They complained that some important issues were either examined in an unduly theoretical manner, or received at best only superficial coverage. Some of these prospective teachers said that they felt ill-equipped to deal with so-called racial incidents, or expressed concern that their knowledge of ethnic differences in religion, culture and lifestyle remained scant. Others endorsed the Swann Committee's recommendations that all student teachers should have the opportunity of gaining practical experience in multiracial schools, or emphasized the need for ethnic minorities to play a more prominent role in initial training:

All students should have a TP (teaching practice) in a multiracial school.

(Male, BEd, junior)

Experience of a multicultural school, via films or actual observation and teaching.

(Male , BEd, secondary)

People with experience (direct experience) of multicultural education should be brought in to talk.

(Female, PGCE, first)

More outside speakers – especially representatives from ethnic minority groups – so that we can have many different points of view; many of us are not sufficiently informed to be able to make judgements on the content of a lecture.

(Female, BEd, infant)

> More contact with teachers working in multicultural situations.
>> (Male, BEd, secondary)

The shortcomings of IT provision in antiracist and multicultural education have also been highlighted by Martin Tracy (1986) in his survey of BEd courses in 29 'public sector' institutions. Employing the CNAA (1984) guidelines as a yardstick, he reported:

> the data from the survey suggests that the degree of take-up of the CNAA suggestions is, as yet, sporadic and slow.
>> (Tracy, 1986, p. 71)

Tracy found that despite the apparently widespread endorsement of 'permeation' as a principle, just 11 of the 29 institutions approached during the survey emphasized the importance of encouraging 'a critical approach to cultural bias, prejudice and stereotyping'. In view of the evidence on the prevalence of racism among young people and children in predominantly or wholly white areas (e.g., Mould 1987; Carrington *et al.*, 1987), his finding that institutions in such areas continue to give relatively low priority to 'issues associated with inequality and discrimination', is especially disturbing.

Some steps are already being taken to tackle antiracist and multicultural education on IT courses in a more practical manner. Ranjit Arora's (1986a) case study of Bradford and Ilkley College, for example, has shown how institutions in ethnically mixed areas might deal with a complex issue such as 'permeation' and provide 'a multi-cultural inner-city perspective on the curriculum' through more extensive involvement with local communities. At the college, all staff and students associated with the BEd degree not only have regular contacts with multiracial schools, but these experiences form an integral part of a range of core and optional studies which seek to develop 'an understanding of British society and the position of ethnic minorities therein'. In common with other studies (discussed below), Arora contends that the attitudes of *some* experienced teachers continue to act as a constraint upon such collaborative ventures.

> The schools did not always share the College's assumptions and beliefs, and indeed racist attitudes in some schools prevented them from participating in the process of teacher training.
>> (Arora, 1986a)

The need for INSET

Although we accept the arguments of Swann and others about the particular role of INSET in the implementation of antiracist and multicultural education, we would not want to be seen as undervaluing the actual or potential contribution of IT. Nor would we want to be seen as endorsing the commensense view that 'teaching cannot be learnt or taught in training institutions, but can only be mastered [sic] on the job' (Atkinson and Delamont, 1985). However, the available evidence on student teachers' and serving teachers' attitudes towards these innovations suggests that more concerted action is required at INSET level: many serving teachers continue to embrace assimilationist or integrationist philosophies and remain either indifferent, or antipathetic, towards contemporary policies (cf., Keel, 1987a; Lee, 1987; Taylor, 1986; Troyna and Ball, 1985).

Not surprisingly, in the light of Tracy's (1986) observations, among others, these views would seem to be especially prevalent in wholly or predominantly white areas. As Bill Taylor found in his appraisal of teachers' responses to antiracist and multicultural education in the south-west of England:

> The idea that immigrants needed compensatory education prevailed nationally in the mid-1960s; it is far from unknown in non-contact areas in the late 1980s. While many teachers would subscribe to the currently fashionable view that every British child needs to be taught to respect the country's various cultures, both teachers and parents in predominantly white regions are still cocooned in their cultural homogeneity.
>
> (Taylor, 1986, p. 80)

He goes on to argue that whereas the 'majority view' of these policies 'in most all-white schools remains one of indifference', this could be 'less to do with racial attitudes than with other priorities being perceived as more pressing'.

Anachronistic (and inadequate) perceptions of the role of the school in a multiracial and multiethnic society are not, of course, solely confined to 'regions still cocooned in their cultural homogeneity'. As Don Lee remarked, in his recent evaluation of North Bedfordshire's INSET strategy: 'integrationist and special education notions' about multicultural education still persist among teachers and heads. Commenting on this, he notes, somewhat ironically:

'In time', minority ethnic group pupils would, surely, learn to 'fit in' and white teachers' and pupils' ethnocentric attitudes, if actually recognised as such, would soon change for the better.

(Lee, 1987, p. 36)

In view of the key role of the headteacher as an 'agent of change' in schools, Lee's observations are especially disconcerting.

Further evidence of the need for more effective INSET provision in antiracist and multicultural education is provided by Barry Troyna and Wendy Ball's (1985) survey in 'Milltown'. Operating on the premise that if a policy is to have any chance of success in a school then it must have the approval of the headteacher, they interviewed the heads of 71 schools (both primary and secondary), asking them to describe their responses to the local authority's multicultural education policy. Whereas nearly all of the heads were aware of the existence of the policy and a sizeable majority (64) said they were 'broadly in favour of it', 24 nevertheless admitted that they had ignored the recommendations for action. Again, non-involvement was largely restricted to schools in predominantly white areas. In the remaining schools, the most common response to the policy has been to reappraise aspects of the formal (rather than hidden) curriculum to ensure that different lifestyles and cultures were adequately represented. Whereas some schools had taken steps to expunge racist and ethnocentric books and teaching materials, or had made curricular provision which sought 'to acquaint pupils with other cultures', only a few had 'taken steps to encourage the infusion of the philosophy into all aspects of the formal curriculum', or had placed the issue of racism 'firmly on the agenda for discussion' (Troyna and Ball, 1985, p. 14). To account for the headteachers' differentiated response to the policy, Troyna and Ball indicated that it was often seen as 'politically inspired' and 'potentially divisive'. In their view, the impact of the policy on schools would have been greater had the staff concerned been given a more comprehensive and coherent statement of its rationale, and more guidance about its implementation. Finally, the research showed that some head-teachers had continued to embrace an assimilationist position because of their limited contact with 'multicultural matters, either in their initial training or in their teaching capacities'.

In view of the frequent allegations in the national media and political fora about bias and indoctrination in schools, and the prevailing image of antiracist and multicultural education as one of the 'loony tunes' of the Left, it is not surprising that many teachers tend to look upon these initiatives as 'politically inspired' and 'potentially divisive'. As Patricia Keel (1987b) has noted, when reflecting on her experience as an action-researcher (in two primary schools in Newcastle upon Tyne):

> It was evident from contact with teachers in both schools that there was a distrust of the underlying 'politics' of multicultural education. Moreover, it was noticeable that those who readily took on the principles of multicultural education, including its antiracist core, tended to be those who might be described as being less conservative, and more inclined towards political and social change that might bring about greater social justice and equality across boundaries of sex, class and ethnicity.
>
> (Keel, 1987b, p. 129)

As we have already indicated (see Chapter 2), many primary school teachers would not fall within Keel's latter category. For them, contentious and 'taboo' topics, such as 'race', class and gender, would normally be eschewed as being beyond the pupils' grasp and even beyond the pale.

Rethinking teacher education

Commenting on the prevailing *zeitgeist* in teacher education, Margaret Sutherland (1985, p. 22) has remarked:

> We have to recognise that when it comes to teacher education, theory tends to have a bad name. It is often said to be divorced from what happens in school, to waste the time of student-teachers and leave them longing for more practically-orientated courses: so the trend is to concentrate on the day-to-day activities of the classroom and give students more and more teaching practice, more contact with teachers, more discussion of control and more class management. But the more insidious danger at present is that in so many cases teacher educators are not quite sure what theory of education is.

Sutherland goes on to claim (p.227) that if one were to ask a group of PGCE students about indoctrination

> they will, almost without exception, assert that indoctrination is a Bad Thing: they are enthusiastic supporters of the view that each child must be encouraged to think for himself/herself. But for what reasons are they opposed to indoctrination? What precisely do they mean by it? Why do they believe children – or adults – to be capable of thinking out all sorts of things – ways of behaving, duties to others, scientific knowledge – for themselves? In what conditions? Are they really willing to accept any conclusions (however stupid or reactionary) thus arrived at by the children or others? Further discussion may reveal that various students have simply made an acceptant response to the indoctrination of the media on this point.

Sutherland is right to argue that if student teachers (or indeed qualified staff) are to develop effective classroom strategies for handling controversial subject matter, then it is essential that they have some understanding of the *concept of indoctrination* and, more generally, of the *process* of educational transmission (cf., Young, 1984). Perhaps some of the unease surrounding the implementation of antiracist and multicultural education might be allayed if IT and INSET were to give more attention to these issues. Certainly, the findings of Keel, Troyna and Ball (among others) indicate the need for such measures. Furthermore, consideration of the available evidence on indoctrination (referred to in Chapter 2) may also help to dispel this unease by showing that much of this criticism is ill-founded.

In addition, it may be necessary for IT and INSET courses to provide prospective and serving teachers with further opportunities to reflect upon and reappraise their *other* taken-for-granted assumptions about discussing controversial issues, particularly with younger children. As we have argued throughout this book, no teaching can be effective unless it makes contact with children's existing knowledge and understanding. If, for example, appropriate curricular strategies are to be devised to reduce individual racism, or to explore other topics related to human rights, social justice or power, then some account must be taken of the following: the development of racial awareness and other forms of collective identity; the process of political and moral socialization (including attitude formation and change); age-related and spatial variations in children's conceptions of racism, sexism and other forms of discrimination. As well as helping to ensure a better 'match' between curricular provision and children's needs, reflection upon the literature under consideration may help to dispel any erroneous beliefs about *inter alia* children's degree of socio-political and moral *sophistication* and ability to *cope* with such provision.

Teaching styles and teacher education

Whether teacher education institutions (especially at IT level) always provide an appropriate pedagogical environment for exploring controversial issues must, however, remain open to question. We have repeatedly called for measures to democratize teaching and learning, and stressed the importance of abandoning excessively didactic 'transmissionist' forms of pedagogy in schools. Yet, as Roland Meighan and Clive Harber (1986, p.167) have claimed:

> Most initial teacher training courses fail to introduce students to the non-authoritarian alternatives of autonomous and democratic approaches to education, either in debate or in the methods practised.

In support of this claim, they cite the HMI report *Teacher Training and the Secondary School*, which drew attention to: the heavy dependence on 'the set lecture with the ensuing tutorial almost equally dominated by the tutor'; and note-taking, passive listening and restricted reading. 'Practice of this kind', according to the report, transmits to the students 'a clear message about the roles of teacher and learner' (DES, 1981, pp. 11–12).

A similar criticism of IT has been made by Jon Nixon (1985) who focuses on the hierarchical relationship between teacher education institutions and the schools (rather than between lecturers and student teachers). Commenting on the increasing contribution made by practising teachers to IT (which, in part, has arisen as a result of the demands of accreditation), he asserts that 'effective curriculum development must build upon genuine collaboration'. He notes, however, that: 'the notion of collaboration can have little significance until the underlying asymmetry between professionals is acknowledged' (p. 154).

We now assess various attempts to promote antiracist and multicultural education through such collaboration, giving particular attention to the importance of action research in INSET.

Action research and INSET

The relationship between teacher education institutions and schools which Arora (1986a) describes in her case study can be extended to include other types of liaison: for example, teacher educators/ researchers working alongside experienced staff in schools, collaborating with them to devise, implement and monitor antiracist, multicultural initiatives. This model underpinned our own work in Denby Dock Middle School and Oldtown Primary School. It has also informed the work of Philip Cohen (1987), Colin Biott, James Lynch and Wendy Robertson (1984), and Patricia Keel (1987b), among others.

Cohen's intervention, which took place in two London primary schools, aimed 'to negotiate the transition from a research-led to a teacher-led initiative, not simply to disseminate ideas' (Cohen, 1987, p. 19). Teachers, youth and community workers participated in an eight week course which, in addition to providing an introduction to prejudice-reduction techniques, enabled members of the group 'to bring into play their unique amalgam of knowledge and experience *and* to relate back the pilot work to their own immediate situation within the classroom and community' (p. 21). The course evaluation revealed a need for: school-focused INSET 'targeted' at strategic teachers; a regular inter-disciplinary forum where teachers and youth workers could meet to discuss race-relations; and the production of accessible INSET and school materials to improve the dissemination, adoption and implementation of the innovation.

Biott and his colleagues (1984) are also committed to the notion of the 'teacher-as-researcher' and to a collaborative approach to INSET. They describe their work in the north east of England, a region with a relatively small black population. Concerned with the diffidence shown by teachers in such areas towards antiracist and multicultural education, they underline the importance of developing 'a system of practical support' in schools which avoids 'convenience recipes' and 'ready-made panaceas'. Particular emphasis is given to the use of 'collaborative discussion' as a means of getting staff to reflect critically on their own professional experiences. Recognizing that the criteria for judging implementation must take account of both regional variations and differences between schools in commitment, the authors in question contend that:

> the dilemmas, which multicultural education evokes for individual schools, should be much more widely discussed, the ideas of people who have found the answers to problems of implementation should be *tested through enquiry for their appropriateness in each setting*. (Emphasis added.)
>
> (Biott *et al.*, 1984, p. 40)

Such discussions have revealed that when teachers lack confidence in their own knowledge of 'race' and ethnicity, they often accord greater priority to curriculum content rather than process. According to Keel, many teachers currently feel that they are expected to have

> at their fingertips, a vast encyclopaedic knowledge of all cultures, which their own education certainly did not give them: 'I think that one reason why some teachers don't go into things is that they don't really know... Ignorance... and you know the other side of it is that people do not always feel confident that they have the policy clearly enough in their mind to know what to do.'
>
> (Keel, 1987b, p. 139)

The primary teachers approached during her action research also expressed concern about the ability of younger children to cope with materials which may seem to be 'remote and foreign to their experience'. To dispel such inhibitions and apprehensions, Keel urges staff to monitor carefully pupils' responses to antiracist and multicultural initiatives, especially in predominantly white areas. To facilitate a more reflective approach to curriculum development, she calls (p. 146) for INSET provision in small-scale research and evaluation:

> Teachers... should be encouraged to collaborate within school and perhaps across schools, to put innovatory measures to

rigorous test. In groups they could look at existing curriculum against consideration of multicultural principles and arrive at areas for possible innovation. Having specific objectives for action, they would monitor action taken, making notes, recordings, and so on, for the collection of data. They might then be in a position to analyse and evaluate the experiment. They might be offered the facility of pooling reports for a publication to be circulated in local schools and further afield.

Perhaps some of these 'basic tools for research' should be provided at the IT stage. Hopefully such an intervention would serve to highlight early on in the young teacher's career the *relevance*, rather than the limitations, of theory, and the shortcomings of common-sense perceptions of educational practice.

INSET and curriculum change

In this chapter, we have argued that a number of benefits may derive from a whole-school approach to antiracist and multicultural education. In particular, we have suggested that the collegial and democratic ethos associated with such an approach would enable staff to reflect upon and share their perceptions of the innovation and its implementation. As Lawrence Stenhouse (1975, p. 166) has noted:

> The power of the individual teacher is limited. Without his [sic] strengths, the betterment of schools can never be achieved; but the strengths of individuals are not effective unless they are co-ordinated and supported. The primary unit of co-ordination and support is the school.

The failure of antiracists and multiculturalists to acknowledge the importance of whole-school and other strategies involved in the change process has led many teachers to adopt an attitude of indifference or hostility to these innovations (cf., Burtonwood, 1986). However, in advocating a collaborative school-based approach to INSET, we recognize the attendant dangers of parochialism. To surmount these, INSET should ideally have an 'off-site' as well as an 'on-site' element. According to Nixon (1985, p. 166):

> In order to develop professionally, teachers need to be able to stand back from the immediate concerns of schooling, to adopt a *theoretical* perspective, to talk with colleagues from other schools and sectors of the education service, to read. Off-site inservice provision can offer them the opportunity of participating in these more *reflective* activities. (Emphasis added.)

An interesting example of such 'off-site' INSET provision is offered by Carl and Gloria Grant's (1985) work in the United States. The two-week residential course evaluated in their study was holistic in its concerns and orientation; it not only addressed participants' racial attitudes and beliefs but also addressed questions relating to gender, class, age and handicap. As well as attempting to influence this range of attitudes, the course aimed to provide participants with the skills to develop, implement and evaluate a whole-school policy dealing with prejudice reduction. To increase the effectiveness of the intervention, a so-called 'buddy system' was employed. The course participants comprised ten groups, each having three members (two teachers and a principal) drawn from the same school.

The course was divided into three phases: 'awareness', 'acceptance' and 'affirmation'. The 'awareness phase' included discussions and 'experiences with the appropriate materials'. The 'acceptance phase' sought to increase the participants' understanding of the process of differentiation, stereotyping and a variety of forms of inequality. The 'affirmation phase' focused on the development, implementation and evaluation of a whole-school policy. Employing a Likert scale to assess participants' attitudes to 'race', sex, handicap, class and age, Grant and Grant found that overall the initiative had a 'positive effect'. However, they noted that 'ethnic stereotyping seems very difficult to eliminate, and, of the five isms [sic] addressed in the Institute, participants had the greatest difficulty working with classism' (Grant and Grant 1985, p. 17). The authors suggested that various factors could have contributed to the observed changes in racial attitude. For example, each participant was assigned to a room with a member of another ethnic group.

Most importantly, however, participants were encouraged to 'discuss racial and class problems openly, without threat of intimidation'.

The success of Grant and Grant's intervention in encouraging participants to talk openly and in a relaxed manner about various 'taboo' issues, contrasts markedly with many Racism Awareness Training programmes.

Racism awareness training

Although there is considerable controversy about the validity and effectiveness of Racism Awareness Training (e.g., Gurnah, 1984; Sivanandan, 1985; Swann Report, 1985), it nevertheless remains prevalent in in-service teacher education. Racism Awareness Training (RAT) was first developed in the United States by Judy Katz (1978). Based on the conception of racism as 'prejudice plus power', which we criticized in Chapter 1, the focus of RAT programmes is the racial attitudes and beliefs of white people. The programmes, which tend to be intensive – often lasting at least two days – utilize a variety of experiential techniques (e.g., role play, brainstorming, self-reflexive and analytic group work), and attempt to get participants to scrutinize and disclose their feelings and prejudices about black people. One or two trainers, who can be either black or white, normally act as 'facilitators' during the group sessions.

Leaving aside its conceptual limitations, RAT has been criticized on various substantive grounds. Chris Gaine (1987), for example, has argued that such programmes are more likely to reinforce rather than obviate personal racism because 'People do not learn, or change attitudes, or change actions when they feel attacked, defensive, hostile, angry or guilty' (p. 103). RAT has been similarly disparaged by James Lynch (1987) who has argued that its advocates are not only 'neglectful of the aetiology of current knowledge about prejudice', but espouse a technique which is 'inimical to the very ethic of a multicultural democracy', and which tends to be 'political, confrontational, accusatory and guilt-inducing in its approach' (p. x). In a more circumspect vein, Patricia Keel (1987a, p.118) has pointed out:

> Nationally, there is no evidence that RAT has positive results. Indeed, there is a danger of negative attitudes becoming en-

trenched, especially if those administering the courses are not fully equipped to counter every type of racist thinking. More-over, using black people to speak out about 'the black experience' can prove bewildering and hurtful to them. Their contribution could reinforce prejudice.

While the programmes in question do not appear to provide an appropriate medium for changing racial attitudes, we obviously accept that there is a need for teachers to scrutinize the values and beliefs which underpin their practice.

Increasing the supply of Afro-Caribbean and South Asian teachers

In Chapter 5, we drew attention to the need to recruit more Afro-Car bbean and South Asian teachers, and also argued that if antiracist and multicultural education was to have a significant impact then steps ought to be taken to ensure that those black teachers *already in post* do not continue to be overrepresented in the lower echelons of the profession. As we have indicated, the potential contribution of black lecturers would probably be appreciated by those on initial teacher education courses. They might also provide a 'black perspective' to counter the racism and ethnocentrism referred to above. However, as the Commission for Racial Equality (1986) has shown in its survey of the ethnic backgrounds of students enrolled in BEd, PGCE and other courses leading to qualified teacher status, black people seem to be underrepresented. According to the Commission:

> Overall, taking students of Afro-Caribbean and Asian origins as 'ethnic minority', they made up only 1 in 40 or 2.6% of all students in the relevant groups/courses, compared with an estimated 5.3% of the appropriate age group in the population.
> (Commission for Racial Equality, 1986, Appendix 2, p. 4)

In the absence of data on the students' social origins, it is not possible to determine the extent to which ethnicity or class is the more salient variable (see Hochschild, 1984; Troyna, 1984). Certainly, the data as presented *suggest* that there may be a class effect, in so far as the more socially heterogeneous group – the Asians – participate more extensively than Afro-Caribbeans in IT, especially on the higher status PGCE route. However, if we accept these data, we might then ask what should be done to increase the supply of ethnic minority teachers.

In the CRE report under consideration, as elsewhere, the importance of access courses is stressed. It should be pointed out that such provision is not new. As Nixon has shown, as long ago as 1978, the DES responded to 'public concern over the disproportionately low numbers of teachers from the ethnic minorities in schools' (Nixon, 1985, p. 155) by inviting seven LEAs to set up pilot schemes to establish these courses. He goes on to note that 'special access courses have now established a strong momentum' and 'their range, and the number of staff and students involved in them, have increased significantly since 1978' (p. 156). Nixon shows that controversy continues to surround such provision which seeks to provide an alternative route into teacher education, especially for the mature student lacking formal entry qualifications. It is unlikely that the restrictions imposed by CATE to limit the numbers of entrants to IT of students with 'alternative qualifications' will result in any improvement in this situation (UCET, 1987). However, research such as Michael Connolly's (1985) could serve to take some of the heat out of the debate. His case study has shown that access course students fared no worse on the BEd degree than their peers with conventional credentials.

Of course, teacher education institutions should not rely solely on access courses to boost ethnic minority recruitment. They should, in addition, think in terms of targeting their appeal rather more directly at such groups. Initially, this could involve advertising in media aimed specifically at ethnic minorities as well as, perhaps, forging stronger links with schools in ethnically mixed areas. Attending careers conventions, for example, in these schools could be given much higher priority. The attraction of teacher education for the groups in question may also be enhanced if institutions were not only to formulate and act upon antiracist policies but were to make their stance explicit in the literature sent out to prospective students. It follows, that effective implementation of these policies will necessitate staff development programmes that move beyond existing RAT, day conferences and short courses. As Penelope Manners (1987, p. 130) has argued:

The issues in multicultural education are complex both in essence and in application; they demand thought and discussion over a lengthy period. Day conferences and short courses can do little more than raise questions and offer some guide lines; a continuing programme of staff development is needed, and for this there needs to be an aware and committed management.

The prospects for change

Throughout our analysis we have steered a course between excessive voluntarism, on the one hand, and determinism, on the other. We have eschewed the view of schooling as *nothing more* than a conservative force, functioning inexorably to maintain and repro- duce the status quo. However, we have also taken cognizance of the limitations of educational reform, by arguing that teachers and schools do not operate in a social and political vacuum, and by stressing that their powers to effect change – pedagogical or otherwise – are severely circumscribed. As Richard Hatcher (1987b, p. 4) has contended, in relation to reform directed towards racial equality:

> The *roots* of reform do not lie with individual teachers, or within schools. The reasons for every major educational reform (and Education for Racial Equality is no exception) can be explained primarily in *political* terms, and not in terms of the attitudes and practices of individual teachers. These are largely – but not entirely – consequences, not causes. 'They think they push, but they are pushed.'

These pressures for reform have emanated from various quarters. Although white liberal and radical commentators have had an influence on developments in this sphere, the real impetus for change has come from within the Afro-Caribbean and South Asian com- munities themselves, and has reflected mounting dissatisfaction with an education perceived as either a hindrance to black attain- ment, or as culturally hostile. Although Hatcher is not optimistic about the prospects for antiracist and multicultural education in the present political climate, he nevertheless acknowledges that 'real progress' has been made since the 1970s, even though political pressures have led some LEAs to water down their policies to combat racism.

Despite this, a cursory examination of recent developments in the UK might lead one to this optimistic conclusion: that with the continuing growth of commitment to racial equality (in teacher education institutions, schools, LEAs and at the DES), antiracist and multicultural education will soon become as firmly enshrined in educational practice as in educational rhetoric. Certainly, there has been *some* ostensible change in official attitude towards these innovations. As Sally Tomlinson (1987) has pointed out, the Council for the Accreditation of Teacher Education now requires 'all student teachers to be properly prepared to teach pupils whatever their social, ethnic or cultural background', and multicultural education has been one of the 'national priority areas' for INSET. However, despite these and other hopeful signs, she also shares Hatcher's pessimism about the future of such reforms. According to Tomlinson:

> the political climate of the 1980s is generally unsympathetic and hostile to those citizens perceived as racially and culturally different, and many politicians and public figures have accepted a steady decline into a morally, unjustifiable treatment of minorities in Britain.
>
> (Tomlinson, 1987, p. 103)

In addition to these political constraints, it is likely that the implementation of the National Curriculum will serve to stifle the development of educational initiatives to promote racial (and social) justice. The operation of 'market forces' and 'league tables' of school test results may encourage public desire for uniformity and make it more difficult for racial and ethnic differences to be accepted. Social and affective goals in education will not only remain subordinate to academic ones but, in all probability, will be further relegated to the peripheries. In primary schools, the increased emphasis on testing and assessment may serve to deter staff from experimenting with more democratic styles of teaching and learning. As we have shown, unless such pedagogical changes occur, lessons which aim to foster the development of open-mindedness and stimulate a respect for human rights, will be likely to fall on deaf ears.

References

ALEXANDER, R.J. (1984). *Primary Teaching*, London: Holt, Rinehart and Winston.

ALLPORT, G.W. (1954). *The Nature of Prejudice*, Cambridge, Mass.: Addison-Wesley.

ARORA, R. (1986a). 'Initial teacher training (a case study of a decade of change in Bradford)'. In: ARORA, R. and DUNCAN, C. (Eds) *Multicultural Education – Towards Good Practice*. London: Routledge and Kegan Paul.

ARORA, R. (1986b). 'A second language or language for learning?'. In: ARORA, R. and DUNCAN, C. (Eds) *Multicultural Education: Towards Good Practice*. London: Routledge and Kegan Paul.

ASHLEY, B. (1977). *The Trouble with Donovan Croft*. Harmondsworth: Penguin.

ASSOCIATION OF LONDON AUTHORITIES (1987). *It's the Way That They Tell 'em*. London: GLC.

ATKINSON, P. and DELAMONT, S. (1985). 'Socialisation into teaching: the research which lost its way', *British Journal of Sociology of Education*, 6, 3, 307–22.

BAGLEY, C., BART, M. and WONG, J. (1978). 'Cognition and scholastic success in West Indian 10–11 year olds in London: a comparative study', *Education Studies*, 4, 1, 7–17.

BALL, W. and TROYNA, B. (1987). 'Resistance, rights and rituals: denominational schools and multicultural education', *Journal of Education Policy*, 2, 1, 15–25.

BANKS, J.A. (1985). 'Reducing prejudice in students: theory, research and strategies'. In: MOODLEY, K. (Ed.) *Race Relations and Multicultural Education*. Vancouver, BC: University of British Columbia.

162   *'Race' and the Primary School*

BANKS, J.A. (1986). 'Multicultural education and its critics: Britain and the United States'. In: MODGIL, S., VERMA, G., MALLICK, K. and MODGIL, C. (Eds.) *Multicultural Education: the Interminable Debate*. Lewes: Falmer Press.

BARKER, M. (1981). *The New Racism*, London: Junction Books.

BARKER-LUNN, J. (1984). 'Junior school teachers: their methods and practices', *Educational Research*, 26, 3, 178–88.

BERDAN, R. (1981). 'Black English and dialect-fair instruction'. In: MERCER, N. (Ed.) *Language in School and Community*. London: Arnold.

BEST, D.I., WILLIAMS, J.E., CLOUD, J.M., DAVIS, S.W., ROBERTSON, L.S., EDWARDS, J.R., GILES, H. and FOWLES, J. (1977). 'Development of sex-trait stereotypes among young children in the United States, England and Ireland', *Child Development*, 48, 1375–84.

BIOTT, C. (1987). 'Co-operative group work: pupils' and teachers' membership and participation', *Curriculum*, 8, 2, 5–14.

BIOTT, C., LYNCH, J. and ROBERTSON, W. (1984). 'Supporting teachers' own progress towards multicultural education', *Multicultural Teaching*, 2, 3, 39–41.

BLAKE, R, and DENNIS, W. (1943). 'The development of stereotypes concerning the Negro', *Journal of Abnormal and Social Psychology*, 38, 525–31.

BLEASE, D. (1983). 'Teachers' expectations and the self-fulfilling prophecy', *Educational Studies*, 9, 2, 123–9.

BOLTON, E. (1979). 'Education in a multiracial society', *Trends in Education*, 4, Winter, 3–7.

BRAHA, V. and RUTTER, D.R. (1980). 'Friendship choice in a mixed-race primary school', *Educational Studies*, 6, 3, 217–23.

BRANDT, G. (1986). *The Realisation of Antiracist Teaching*. Lewes: Falmer Press.

BRIDGEMAN, B. and SHIPMAN, V.C. (1978). 'Pre-school measures of self-esteem and achievement as predictors of third grade achievement', *Journal of Educational Psychology*, 70, 1, 17–28.

BRIDGES, D. (1986). 'Dealing with controversy in the school curriculum: a philosophical perspective'. In: WELLINGTON, J.J. (Ed.) *Controversial Issues in the Curriculum*. Oxford: Blackwell.

BRIGLEY, S., COATES, P. and NOBLE, H. (1988). '"Taboo" issues in rural schools', *Forum*, 30, 2, 50–55.

BRITTAN, E. (1976). 'Multiracial education 2: teacher opinion on aspects of school life. Part 2: pupils and teachers', *Educational Research*, 18, 3, 182–91.

BROPHY, J. and GOOD, T. (1970). 'Teachers' communication of differential expectations for children's classroom performance: some behavioural data', *Journal of Educational Psychology*, 61, 5, 365–74.

BROWN, C. (1986). *Black and White Britain*. London: Policy Studies Institute.

BROWN, G. and JOHNSON, S. (1971). 'The attribution of behavioural connotations to shaded and white figures by Caucasian children', *British Journal of Social and Clinical Psychology*, 10, 4, 306–12.

BRUNER, J. (1960). *The Process of Education*. New York: Vintage Books.

BRYANT, P. (1974). *Perception and Understanding in Young Children*. London: Methuen.

BRYANT, P. (1984). 'Piaget, teachers and psychologists', *Oxford Review of Education*, 10, 3, 251–9.

BULLIVANT, B.M. (1981). *The Pluralist Dilemma in Education*. Sydney: George Allen and Unwin.

BULLOCK REPORT. GREAT BRITAIN. DEPARTMENT OF EDUCATION AND SCIENCE (1985). *Committee of Inquiry into the Teaching and the Use of English. A Language for Life*. London: HMSO.

BURGESS, C. (1986). 'Tackling racism and sexism in the classroom'. In: GUNDARA, J., JONES, C. and KIMBERLEY, K. (Eds) *Racism, Diversity and Education*. London: Macmillan.

BURGESS, H. (1988). 'Perception of the primary and middle school curriculum'. In: CARRINGTON, B. and TROYNA, B. (Eds.) *Children and Controversial Issues: Strategies for the Early and Middle Years of Schooling*. Lewes: Falmer Press.

BURTONWOOD, N. (1986). 'INSET and multicultural/antiracist education: some reflections on Swann and after', *British Journal of In-Service Education*, 13, 1, 30–35.

CALSYN, R.J, and KENNY, D.A. (1977). 'Self-concept of ability and perceived evaluation of others: cause or effect of academic achievement?', *Journal of Educational Psychology*, 69, 2, 136–45.

CAMPBELL, J. (1986). 'Involving parents in equal opportunities: one school's attempt'. In: *Primary Matters: some Approaches to Equal Opportunities in Primary Schools*. London: ILEA.

CAMPBELL, R. and LAWTON, D. (1970). 'How children see society', *New Society*, 19 November.

CARRINGTON, B. (1981). 'Schooling an underclass: the implications of ethnic differences in attainment', *Durham and Newcastle Research Review*, 9, 47, 293–305.

CARRINGTON, B. (1986). 'Social mobility, ethnicity and sport', *British Journal of Sociology of Education*, 7, 1, 3–18.

CARRINGTON, B., CHIVERS, T. and WILLIAMS, T. (1987). 'Gender, leisure and sport: a case study of young people of South Asian descent', *Leisure Studies*, 6, 3, 265–79.

CARRINGTON, B., MILLWARD, A. and SHORT, G. (1986). 'Schooling in a multiracial society: contrasting perspectives of primary and secondary teachers in training', *Educational Studies*, 12, 1, 17–35.

CARRINGTON, B. and SHORT, G. (1987). 'Breakthrough to political literacy: political education, antiracist teaching and the primary school', *Journal of Education Policy*, 2, 1, 1–13.

CARRINGTON, B. and SHORT, G. (1989). 'Policy or presentation? The psychology of antiracist education', *New Community* (in press).

CARRINGTON, B. and TROYNA, B. (1988). 'Combatting racism through political education'. In: CARRINGTON, B. and TROYNA, B. (Eds) *Children and Controversial Issues: Strategies for the Early and Middle Years of Schooling*. Lewes: Falmer Press.

CARRINGTON, B. and WILLIAMS, T. (1988). 'Patriarchy and ethnicity: the link between school physical education and community leisure activities'. In: EVANS, J. (Ed.) *Teachers, Training and Control in Physical Education*. Lewes: Falmer Press.

CARRINGTON, B. and WOOD, E. (1983) 'Body talk: images of sport in a multiracial school', *Multiracial Education*, 11, 2, 29–38.

CARTER, B. and WILLIAMS, J. (1987). 'Attacking racism in education'. In: TROYNA, B. (Ed.) *Racial Inequality in Education*. London: Tavistock.

CHEVANNES, F. and REEVES, M. (1987). 'The black voluntary school movement'. In: TROYNA, B. (Ed.) *Racial Inequality in Education*. London: Tavistock.

CLARK, K. (1955). *Prejudice and Your Child*. Boston: Beacon Press.

CLARK, K. and CLARK, M. (1939). 'The development of consciousness of self and the emergence of racial identification in Negro preschool children', *Journal of Social Psychology*, SPSSI Bulletin, 10, 591–9.

CLARK, K. and CLARK, M. (1947). 'Racial identification and preference in Negro children'. In: NEWCOMB, T.M. and HARTLEY, E.L. (Eds.) *Readings in Social Psychology*. New York: Holt, Rinehart and Winston.

CLARRICOATES, K. (1980). 'The importance of being Ernest, Emma, Tom, Jane...?'. In: DEEM, R. (Ed.) *Schooling for Women's Work*, London: Routledge and Kegan Paul.

COARD, B. (1971). *How the West Indian Child is Made Educationally Subnormal in the British School System*. London: New Beacon Books.

COHEN, P. (1987). *Reducing Prejudice in the Classroom and Community*. London: PSEC/CME Cultural Studies Project, University of London Institute of Education (mimeo).

COMMISSION FOR RACIAL EQUALITY (1986). *Black Teachers: the Challenge of Increasing the Supply*. London: CRE.

COMMUNITY DEVELOPMENT PROJECT (1977). *Guilding the Ghetto: The State and the Poverty Experiments*. London: CDP.

CONNOLLY, M. (1985). 'Achievement of access and non-access students on a BEd course: addendum', *New Community*, 12, 2, 273–75.

CONNOR, W. (1972). 'Nation-building or nation-destroying?', *World Politics*, 24, 319–55.

CORDER, S.P. (1974). 'The significance of learners' errors'. In: RICHARDS, J.C. (Ed). *Error Analysis: Perspectives on Second Language Acquisition*. London: Longman.

CNAA (COUNCIL FOR NATIONAL ACADEMIC AWARDS) (1984). 'Multicultural education: a discussion paper'. London: CNAA.

CRAFT, M. (1984). 'Education for Diversity'. In: CRAFT, M. (Ed.) *Education and Cultural Pluralism*. Lewes: Falmer Press.

CRAFT, M. and CRAFT, A. (1983). 'The participation of ethnic minority pupils in further and higher education', *Educational Research*, 25, 1, 10–19.

CRONIN, A. (1984). 'Supplementary schools: their role in culture maintenance, identity and underachievement', *New Community*, 11, 3, 256–67.

DAMON, W. (1977). *The Social World of the Child*. San Francisco: Jossey-Bass.

DAVEY, A. (1983). *Learning to be Prejudiced*. London: Edward Arnold.

DAVEY, A. (1987a). 'Inter-ethnic friendship patterns in British schools over three decades', *New Community*, 14, 1/2, 202–9.

DAVEY, A. (1987b). 'Insiders, outsiders and anomalies: a review of studies of identities – a reply to Olivia Foster-Carter', *New Community*, 13, 3, 477–82.

DEEM, R. (Ed.) (1984). *Coeducation Reconsidered*. Milton Keynes: Open University Press.

DES (DEPARTMENT OF EDUCATION AND SCIENCE) (1977). *Education in Schools: a Consultative Document.* Cmnd 6869. London: HMSO.

DES (DEPARTMENT OF EDUCATION AND SCIENCE) (1981). *Teacher Training and the Secondary School.* London: HMSO.

DES (DEPARTMENT OF EDUCATION AND SCIENCE) (1982). *The New Teacher and the School: a Report.* London: HMSO.

DES (DEPARTMENT OF EDUCATION AND SCIENCE) (1983a). *Teaching Quality.* Cmnd 8836. London: HMSO.

DES (DEPARTMENT OF EDUCATION AND SCIENCE) (1983b). *9–13 Middle Schools: an Illustrative Survey.* London: HMSO.

DES (DEPARTMENT OF EDUCATION AND SCIENCE) (1985a). *The Curriculum from 5 to 16.* London: HMSO.

DES (DEPARTMENT OF EDUCATION AND SCIENCE) (1985b). *Statistics of Education: Teachers in Service, England and Wales.* London: HMSO.

DES (DEPARTMENT OF EDUCATION AND SCIENCE) (1986). *Education Act* (No. 22). London: HMSO.

DES (DEPARTMENT OF EDUCATION AND SCIENCE) (1987). *The National Curriculum, 5–16 – A Consultative Document.* London: HMSO.

DICKENSON, M.J. (1988). 'Education for a multicultural society, the historical perspective: the Jewish community in Leeds, 1885–1920', *Educational Administration and History*, 20, 1, 38–53.

DONALDSON, M. (1978). *Children's Minds.* London: Fontana/Collins.

DRIVER, G. (1980). *Beyond Underachievement: Case Studies of English, West Indian and Asian School-leavers at 16-plus.* London: Commission for Racial Equality.

DUNN, D. (1986). 'In service, mis-education'. In: ARORA, R. and DUNCAN, C. (Eds.) *Multicultural Education: Towards Good Practice.* London: Routledge and Kegan Paul.

DUORAJAIYE, M.O.A. (1969). 'Race relations among junior school children', *Educational Research*, 11, 3, 226–8.

EDWARDS, A.D. and FURLONG, V.J. (1978). *The Language of Teaching.* London: Heinemann.

EDWARDS, V. (1983). *Language in Multicultural Classrooms.* London: Batsford Educational.

EGGLESTON, S.J. (1981). 'Present provision in inservice training'. In: CRAFT, M. (Ed.) *Teaching in a Multicultural Society.* Lewes: Falmer Press.

EGGLESTON, S.J., DUNN, R., and PUREWAL, A. (1981). *In-Service Teacher Education in a Multicultural Society.* Keele: University of Keele.

EUROPEAN ECONOMIC COMMUNITY (1977). *Council Directive on the Education of Children of Migrant Workers.* 77/486/EEC, 25 July.

FIGUEROA, P. (1984). 'Minority pupil progress'. In: CRAFT, M. (Ed.) *Education and Cultural Pluralism.* Lewes: Falmer Press.

FITZ-GIBBON, C. (1983). 'Peer-tutoring: a possible method for multiethnic education', *New Community*, 11, 1/2, 160–166.

FLANDERS, N.A. (1970). *Analyzing Teaching Behaviour.* Reading, Mass.: Addison Wesley.

FOSTER-CARTER, O. (1987). 'The Honeyford affair'. In: TROYNA, B, (Ed.) *Racial Inequality in Education.* London: Tavistock.

FOX, D.J. and JORDAN, V.B. (1973). 'Racial preference and identification of black American Chinese and white children', *Genetic Psychology Monographs*, 88, 2, 229–86.

FRANCIS, M. (1984). 'Antiracist teaching in the primary school'. In: STRAKER-WELDS, M. (Ed.) *Education for a Multicultural Society: Case Studies in ILEA Schools.* London: Bell and Hyman.

FRENCH, J. (1986). 'Gender and the classroom', *New Society*, 7, March 1986, 404–6.

FRENCH, P. and FRENCH, J. (1986). *Gender Imbalances in Infant School Classroom Interaction.* Manchester: Equal Opportunities Commission.

GAINE, C. (1987). *No Problem Here: a Practical Approach to Education and Race in White Schools.* London: Hutchinson.

GALTON, M. (1981). 'Teaching groups in the junior school: a neglected art', *School Organisation*, 1, 2, 175–81.

GALTON, M. (1987). 'Change and continuity in the primary school: the research evidence'. *Oxford Review of Education*, 13, 1, 81–93.

GASPER, I. (1985). 'Handling politics in the classroom'. *Teaching Politics*, 14, 1, 41–51.

GELMAN, R. (1978). 'Cognitive development', *Annual Review of Psychology*, 29, 297–332.

GILES, R. and CHERRINGTON, D. (1981). 'Present provision in initial training'. In: CRAFT, M. (Ed.) *Teaching in a Multicultural Society.* Lewes: Falmer Press.

GILL, D. (1983). 'Anti-racist teaching through geography', *Contemporary Issues in Geographical Education*, 1, 1, 34–5.

GOOD, T. (1980). 'Classroom expectations: teacher-pupil interactions'. In: MCMILLAN J. (Ed.) *The Social Psychology of School Learning.* London: Academic Press.

GOODMAN, M. E. (1952). *Race Awareness in Young Children.* Cambridge, Mass.: Addison-Wesley.

GRANT, C. (1973). 'Black studies materials do make a difference', *Journal of Educational Research*, 66, 9, 400–4.

GRANT, C. and GRANT, G. (1985). 'Staff development and education that is multicultural: a study of an in-service institute for teachers and principals', *British Journal of In-service Education*, 12, 1, 6–18.

GREEN, P. (1983). Teachers' influence on the self-concept of pupils of different ethnic origins. Unpublished PhD thesis, University of Durham,

GREENWALD, H.J. and OPPENHEIM, D.B. (1968). 'Reported magnitude of self-misidentification among Negro-children: artifact?', *Journal of Personality and Social Psychology*, 8, 1, 49–52.

GURNAH, A. (1984). The politics of racism awareness training', *Critical Social Policy*, 11, 6–20.

GUTTMANN, J. (1984). 'The relative importance of ethnic origin and study characteristics in the formation of teachers' evaluation', *Research in Education*, 31, 1–10.

HALEY, A. (1968). *The Autobiography of Malcolm X*. Harmondsworth: Penguin.

HALSEY, A.H., HEATH, A.F. and RIDGE, J.M. (1980). *Origins and Destinations*. Oxford: Oxford University Press.

HALSTEAD, J.M. and KHAN-CHEEMA, A. (1987). 'Muslims and worship in the maintained school', *Westminister Studies in Education*, 10, 21–36.

HAMMERSLEY, M. (1981). *Staffroom Racism*, unpublished manuscript.

HANNAN, A. (1985). 'The education and training of teachers and the "multicultural dimensions"', *Multiracial Education*, 13, 1, 19–28.

HARBER, C. (1984). 'Politics and political education 1984', *Educational Review*, 36, 2, 110–120.

HARBER, C. (Ed.) (1987). *Political Education in Britain*. Lewes: Falmer Press.

HARGREAVES, D.H. (1982). *The Challenge for the Comprehensive School: Culture, Curriculum and Community*. London: Routledge and Kegan Paul.

HARWOOD, D. (1985). 'We need political not Political education for 5–13 year olds', *Education 3–13*, 13, 1, 12–17.

HARWOOD, D. (1986). 'To advocate or educate', *Education 3–13*, 14, 1, 51–57.

HATCHER, R. (1987a). 'Race and education: two perspectives for change'. In: TROYNA, B. (Ed.) *Racial Inequality in Education*. London: Tavistock.

HATCHER, R. (1987b). 'Education for racial equality under attack', *Multicultural Teaching*, 5, 3, 4–7.

HEATH, A. and CLIFFORD, P. (1980). 'The seventy thousand hours that Rutter left out', *Oxford Review of Education*, 6, 1, 3–19.

HICKS, D. (1981). 'Images of the world: what do geography text books actually teach about development?', *Cambridge Journal of Education*, 11, 1, 15–35.

HICKS, D. (1987). 'Education for peace: principles into practice', *Cambridge Journal of Education*, 17, 1, 3–12.

HOCHSCHILD, J.L. (1984). *The New American Dilemma: Liberal Democracy and School Desegregation*. New Haven: Yale University Press.

HONEYFORD, R. (1987). 'The Swann fiasco', *The Salisbury Review*, April, 54–6.

HOROWITZ, E.L. (1936). 'Development of attitudes towards Negroes'. In: PROSCHANSKY, H. and SEIDENBERG, B. (Eds.) (1965) *Basic Studies in Social Psychology*. New York: Holt, Rinehart and Winston.

HOROWITZ, E.L. and HOROWITZ, R.E. (1983). 'Development of social attitudes in children', *Sociometry*, 1, 307–38.

HOROWITZ, R.E. (1939). 'Racial aspects of self-identification in nursery school children', *Journal of Psychology*, 7, 91–99.

HOUSE OF COMMONS, Select Committee on Race Relations and Immigration (1973). *Education*, Vols 1–3. London: HMSO.

HOUSE OF COMMONS, Select Committee on Race Relations and Immigration (1977). *The West Indian Community*, Vol. 1, London: HMSO.

HOUSE OF COMMONS, Select Committee on Race Relations and Immigration (1981). *5th Report of the Home Affairs Committee*. London: HMSO.

HRABA, J. and GRANT, G. (1970). 'Black is beautiful: a re-examination of racial identification and preference', *Journal of Personality and Social Psychology*, 16, 3, 398–402.

HUGHES, M. (1975). Egocentricism in pre-school children. Unpublished PhD thesis, Edinburgh University.

HUSBAND, C. (Ed.) (1982). *Race in Britain: Continuity and Change*. London: Hutchinson.

HUSBANDS, C.T. (1983). *Racial Exclusionism and the City: the Urban Support of the National Front*. London: Allen and Unwin.

ILEA (INNER LONDON EDUCATION AUTHORITY) (1986). *The Teaching of Controversial Issues in Schools: Advice from the Inspectorate*, London: ILEA.

JEFFCOATE, R. (1977). 'Children's racial ideas and feelings', *English in Education*, 11, 1, 32–48.

JEFFCOATE, R. (1979). *Positive Image: Towards a Multiracial Curriculum*. London: Chameleon Books/Readers and Writers Publishing Cooperative.

JEFFCOATE, R. (1984). *Ethnic Minorities and Education*. London: Harper and Row.

JEFFS, T. (1988). 'Preparing young people for participatory democracy' In: CARRINGTON B. and TROYNA, B. (Ed.) *Children and Controversial Issues: Strategies for the Early and Middle Years of Schooling..* Lewes: Falmer Press.

JONES, M. (1985). 'Education and racism', *Journal of Philosophy of Education*, 19, 2, 223–34.

KATZ, J. (1978). *White Awareness: Handbook for an Antiracism Training*. Norman, Oklahoma: University of Oklahoma Press.

KATZ, P.A. (1983). 'Developmental foundations of gender and racial attitudes'. In: LEAHY, R.L. (Ed.) *The Child's Construction of Social Inequality*. New York: Academic Press.

KATZNELSON, I. (1973). *Black Men, White Cities*. London: Oxford University Press.

KEEL, P. (1987a). 'An outline of multicultural education development'. In: CHIVERS, T.S. (Ed.) *Race and Culture in Education: Issues Arising from the Swann Committee Report*. Windsor: NFER–NELSON.

KEEL, P. (1987b). 'Action research as a medium for curriculum development'. In: CHIVERS, T.S. (Ed.) *Race and Culture in Education: Issues Arising from the Swann Committee Report*. Windsor: NFER–NELSON.

KING, E. (1986). 'Recent experimental strategies for prejudice in American schools and classrooms', *Journal of Curriculum Studies*, 18, 3, 331–8.

KING, R. (1978). *All Things Bright and Beautiful? A Sociological Study of Infants' Classrooms*. Chichester: Wiley.

KIRP, D. (1979). *Doing Good by Doing Little*. Berkeley, California: University of California Press.

KLEIN, G. (1985). *Reading into Racism: Bias in Children's Literature and Learning Materials*. London: Routledge and Kegan Paul.

KLEIN, G. (1986). 'The role of the school library in multicultural education'. In: GUNDARA, J., JONES, C. and KIMBERLEY, K. (Eds.) *Racism, Diversity and Education*. London: Macmillan.

KOWALCZEWSKI, P. (1982). 'Race and education: racism, diversity and equality, implications for multicultural education', *Oxford Review of Education*, 8, 2, 145–60.

KUHN, D., NASH, S.C. and BRUCKEN, L. (1978). 'Sex role concepts of two and three year olds', *Child Development*, 49, 445–51.

KYSEL, F. (1988). 'Ethnic background and examination results', *Educational Research*, 30, 2, 83–90.

LANE, N.R. and LANE, S.R. (1986). 'Rationality, self-esteem and autonomy through collaborative enquiry', *Oxford Review of Education*, 12, 3, 263–275.

LaPIERE, R.T. (1934). 'Attitudes versus actions', *Social Forces*, 13, 230–37.

LASKER, B. (1929). *Race Attitudes in Children*. New York: Holt.

LEACOCK, E. (1971). *The Culture of Poverty: a Critique*. New York: Simon and Schuster.

LEAHY, R.L. (1983). 'The development of the conception of social class'. In: LEAHY, R.L. (Ed.) *The Child's Construction of Social Inequality*. New York: Academic Press.

LEE, D. (1987). 'Towards a coherent strategy for INSET: a systematic approach to implementation', *Multicultural Teaching*, 5, 3, 36–8.

LEE, V., LEE, J. and PEARSON, M. (1987). 'Stories children tell'. In: POLLARD, A. (Ed.) *Children and their Primary Schools: a New Perspective*. Lewes: Falmer Press.

LEICESTER, M. (1986). 'Multicultural curriculum or antiracist education: denying the gulf', *Multicultural Teaching*, 4, 2, 4–7.

LINGUISTIC MINORITIES PROJECT (1985). *The Other Languages of England*. London: Routledge and Kegan Paul.

LITTLE, A. and WILLEY, R. (1981). *Multiethnic Education: the Way Forward*. York: Longman/Schools Council.

LYNCH, J. (1983). *The Multicultural Curriculum*. London: Batsford.

LYNCH, J. (1986a). *Multicultural Education: Principles and Practice*. London: Routledge and Kegan Paul.

LYNCH, J. (1986b). 'An initial typology of perspectives on staff development for multicultural teacher education'. In: MODGIL, S., VERMA, G. MALLICK, K. and MODGIL, C. (Eds.) *Multicultural Education: the Interminable Debate*. Lewes: Falmer Press.

LYNCH, J. (1987). *Prejudice Reduction and the Schools*. London: Cassell.

MABEY, C. (1981). *'Black British literacy: a study of reading attainment of London black children from 8 to 15 years'*, Educational Research, 23, 2, 83–95.

MADGE, N. (1976). 'Context and the expressed ethnic preferences of infant school children', *Journal of Child Psychology and Psychiatry*, 17, 4, 337–44.

MANNERS, P. (1987). 'FE teacher education in a multi-ethnic society', *British Journal of Inservice Education*, 13, 3, 128–31.

MARKS, J. (1986). '"Antiracism" – revolution not education'. In: PALMER, F. (Ed.) *Antiracism – an Assault on Education and Value*. London: Sherwood Press.

MARLAND, M. (1986). 'Towards a curriculum policy for a multi-lingual world', *British Journal of Language Teaching*, 24, 3, 123–38.

McCANDLESS, B.R. and HOYT, J.J. (1961). 'Sex, ethnicity and play preference of pre-school children', *Journal of Abnormal and Social Psychology*, 62, 683–5.

McLUHAN, M. (1964). *Understanding Media: the Extensions of Man*. London: Routlege and Kegan Paul.

MEIGHAN, R. and HARBER, C. (1986). 'Democratic learning in teacher education: a review of experience at one institution', *Journal of Education for Teaching*, 12, 2, 163–72.

MENTER, I. (1987). 'Evaluating teacher education: some notes on an anti-racist programme for BEd students', *Multicultural Teaching*, 5, 3, 39–41.

MENTER, I. (1988). 'Antiracist action: setting an agenda for teacher education', *Forum*, 30, 3, 80–2.

MERTON, R. (1949). *Social Theory and Social Structure*. New York: Free Press.

MILMAN, D. (1984). 'Childeric school: developing a multicultural policy'. In: STRAKER-WELDS, M. (Ed.) *Education for a Multicultural Society: Case Studies in ILEA Schools*. London: Bell and Hyman.

MILNER, D. (1982). 'Multiculturalism: the "acceptable face of multi-racial education"', *New Community*, 10, 1, 72–5.

MILNER, D. (1983). *Children and Race: Ten Years On*. London: Ward Lock Educational.

MONTE, H. (1986). 'Some of my best friends are', *History and Social Sciences: Teachers Centre Review*, 6, 1, 23–6.

MORENO, J.L. (1934). *Who Shall Survive?* Washington: Nervous and Mental Disorders Publishing Co.

MORLAND, J.K. (1962). 'Racial acceptance and preference of nursery school children in a southern city', *Merril-Palmer Quarterly*, 8, 4, 271–80.

MORTIMORE, J. and BLACKSTONE, T. (1982). *Disadvantage and Education*. London: Heinemann.

MOULD, W. (1987). 'The Swann Report: an LEA response'. In: CHIVERS, T.S. (Ed.) *Race and Culture in Education: Issues Arising from the Swann Committee Report*. Windsor: NFER-NELSON.

MULLARD, C. (1982). 'Multiracial education: from assimilation to cultural pluralism'. In: TIERNEY, J. (Ed.) *Race, Migration and Schooling*. London: Holt, Rinehart and Winston.

MULLARD, C., BONNICK, L. and KING, B. (1983). *Process, Problem and Prognosis – a Survey of Local Education Authorities' Multicultural Education Policies and Practices*. London: University of London Institute of Education.

MULVANEY, M. (1984). 'The impact of an antiracist policy on the school community'. In: STRAKER-WELDS, M. (Ed.) *Education for a Multicultural Society: Case Studies in ILEA Schools*. London: Bell and Hyman.

NAGUIB, M. (1985). 'Racism as an aspect of the Swann report: a black perspective', *Multicultural Teaching*, 4, 2, 8–10.

NIXON, J. (1985). *A Teacher's Guide to Multicultural Education*. London: Blackwell.

PALARDY, J.M. (1969). 'What teachers believe – what children achieve', *Elementary School Journal*, 69, 370–4.

PALMER, F. (1986). 'Introduction'. In: PALMER, F. (Ed.) *Antiracism – an Assault on Education and Value*. London: Sherwood Press.

PAREKH, B. (1985). 'Background to the West Indian tragedy', *The Times Educational Supplement*, 22 March.

PATTERSON, S. (1985). 'Random samplings from Swann', *New Community*, 12, 2, 239–48.

PHILLIPS, G. (1983). 'Taking political autonomy seriously: a reply to Ian Gregory', *Westminster Studies in Education*, 6, 13–20.

PIAGET, J. (1926). *The Language and Thought of the Child*. London: Routledge and Kegan Paul.

PIAGET, J. (1932). *The Moral Judgment of the Child*. London: Routledge and Kegan Paul.

POLLARD, A. and TANN, S. (1987). *Reflective Teaching in the Primary School*. London: Cassell.

PUSHKIN, I (1967). A study of ethnic choice in the play of young children in three London districts. Unpublished PhD thesis, University of London.

RADKE, M., SUTHERLAND, J. and ROSENBERG, P. (1950). 'Racial attitudes of children', *Sociometry*, 13, 154–71.

RAHMAN, A. (1977). *The Times Educational Supplement*, 1 April.

RAMPTON REPORT. GREAT BRITAIN. DEPARTMENT OF EDUCATION AND SCIENCE (1981). *West Indian Children in Our Schools*. Cmnd 8723. London: HMSO.

REDBRIDGE COMMUNITY RELATIONS COUNCIL (1978). *Cause for Concern*. London: Redbridge CRC.

REEVES, F. and CHEVANNES, M. (1981). 'The underachievement of Rampton', *Multiracial Education*, 12, 1, 35–42.

REID, A. (1985). 'An outsider's view of political education in England: past and present?', *Teaching Politics*, 14, 1, 13–18.

RICE, I. (1987). 'Racism and reading schemes: 1986, the current situation', *Reading*, 21, 2, 92–8.

RICHARDS, C. (1986). 'Antiracist initiatives', *Screen*, 27, 5, 74–9.

RICHARDSON, R. (1988). 'The right approach', *New Internationalist*, February, p. 11.

RICHMOND, A. (1985). 'Before and after the Swann Report', *New Community*, 12, 2, 225–7.

ROKEACH, M. (1960). *The Open and Closed Mind*. New York: Basic Books.

ROSE, E.J.B. *et al.* (1969). *Colour and Citizenship: a Report on British Race Relations*. London: Oxford University Press.

ROSE, S. (1979). 'Race, intelligence and education', *New Community*, 7, 2, 280–3.

ROSENTHAL, R. and JACOBSON, L. (1968). *Pygmalion in the Classroom*. New York: Holt, Rinehart and Winston.

ROSS, A. (1984). 'Developing political concepts and skills in the primary school', *Educational Review*, 36, 2, 131–9.

ROWLEY, K.G. (1968). 'Sociometric study of friendship choices among English and immigrant children', *Educational Research*, 10, 2, 145–8.

RUBOVITZ, P.C. and MAEHR, M.L. (1973). 'Pygmalion black and white', *Journal of Personality and Social Psychology*, 25, 2, 210–8.

RUDDOCK, J. and PLASKOW, M. (1985). 'Bring back the neutral chairman', *Times Educational Supplement*, 21 June.

RUTTER, M., MAUGHAN, B., MORTIMORE, P. and OUSTON, J. with SMITH, A. (1979). *Fifteen Thousand Hours: Secondary Schools and their Effects on Children*. London: Open Books.

RUTTER, M., YULE, W., BERGER, M., MORTON, J. and BAGLEY, C. (1974). 'Children of West Indian immigrants – 1: rates of behavioural deviance and of psychiatric disorder', *Journal of Child Psychology and Psychiatry*, 15, 4, 241–62.

SACHS, J. (1986). 'Putting culture back into multicultural education', *New Community*, 13, 2, 195–9.

SALMON, P. and CLAIRE, H. (1984). *Classroom Collaboration*. London: Routledge and Kegan Paul.

SAUNDERS, M. (1982). *Multicultural Teaching: a Guide for the Classroom*. London: McGraw Hill.

SCARR, S., CAPARULO, B., BERNADO, M. and TOWER, R. (1983). 'Developmental status and school achievements of minority and non-minority children from birth to 18 years in a British midlands town', *British Journal of Developmental Psychology*, 1, 1, 31–48.

SELINKER, L. (1972). 'Interlanguage', *International Review of Applied Linguistics*, 10, 3, 209–31.

SHERIF, M., HARVEY, O.J., WHITE, B.J., HOOD, W.R. and SHERIF, C. (1954). *Experimental Study of Positive and Negative Intergroup Attitudes between Experimentally Produced Groups: Robbers Cave Study*. Norman, Oklahoma: University of Oklahoma Press.

SHORT, G. (1981). 'Racial attitudes among Caucasian children: an empirical study of Allport's "total rejection" hypothesis', *Educational Studies*, 7, 2, 197–205.

SHORT, G. (1983). 'Rampton revisited: a study of racial stereotypes in the primary school', *The Durham and Newcastle Research Review*, 10, 51, 82–6.

SHORT, G. (1985). 'Teacher expectation and West Indian underachievement', *Educational Research*, 27, 2, 95–101.

SHORT, G. and CARRINGTON, B. (1987). 'Towards an antiracist initiative in the all-white primary school'. In: POLLARD, A. (Ed.) *Children and their Primary Schools: a New Perspective*. Lewes: Falmer Press.

SINGH, B. (1988). 'The teaching of controversial issues: the problems of the neutral-chair approach'. In: CARRINGTON, B. and TROYNA, B. (Eds.) *Children and Controversial Issues: Strategies for the Early and Middle Years of Schooling*. Lewes: Falmer Press.

SINGLETON, L.C. and ASHER, S.R. (1977). 'Peer preferences and social interaction among third-grade children in an integrated school district', *Journal of Educational Psychology*, 69, 4, 330–6.

SIVANANDAN, A. (1976). *Race, Class and the State: the Black Experience in Britain*. London: Institute of Race Relations.

SIVANANDAN, A. (1985). 'RAT and the degradation of the black struggle', *Race and Class*, 26, 4, 1–33.

SLATER, J. (1979). 'An HMI perspective on peace education'. In: *Educating People*. London: The National Council of Women of Great Britain.

SLAVIN, R. (1979). 'Integrating the desegregated classroom: actions speak louder than words',*Educational Leadership*, 36, 5, 322–24.

SLAVIN, R. (1983). *Co-operative Learning*. London: Methuen.

STENHOUSE, L. (1970). *The Humanities Project: an Introduction*. London: Heinemann.

STENHOUSE, L. (1975). *An Introduction to Curriculum Research and Development*, London: Heinemann.

STENHOUSE, L. and VERMA, K. (1981). 'Educational procedures and attitudinal objectives: a paradox', *Journal of Curriculum Studies*, 13, 4, 329–37.

STEVENS, O. (1982). *Children Talking Politics: Political Learning in Childhood*. Oxford: Martin Robertson.

STONE, M. (1981). *The Education of the Black Child in Britain: the Myth of Multiracial Education*. London: Fontana.

STONES, R. (1983). *Pour Out the Cocoa Janet: Sexism in Children's Books*. York: Longman/Schools Council.

STRADLING, R., NOCTOR, M. and BAINS, B. (1984). *Teaching Controversial Issues*. London: Edward Arnold.

STREET-PORTER, R. (1978). *Race, Children and the Cities*. Unit E361. Milton Keynes: Open University Press.

SUTHERLAND, M. (1985). 'The place of theory of education in teacher education', *British Journal of Educational Studies*, 33, 3, 222–34.

SUTTON, A. (1983). 'An introduction to Soviet developmental psychology'. In: MEADOWS, S. (Ed.) *Developing Thinking*. London: Methuen.

SWANN REPORT. GREAT BRITAIN. DEPARTMENT OF EDUCATION AND SCIENCE (1985). *Committee of Inquiry into the Education of Children from Ethnic Minority Groups. Education for All*. Cmnd 9453. London: HMSO.

TANNA, K. (1985). 'Opening the black box', *The Times Educational Supplement*, 20 September.

TAYLOR, B. (1986). 'Antiracist education in non-contact areas: the need for a gentle approach', *New Community*, 13, 2, 177–84.

TAYLOR, M. (1981). *Caught Between – a Review of Research into the Education of Pupils of West Indian Origin*. Windsor: NFER-NELSON.

TAYLOR, M. and HEGARTY, S. (1985) *The Best of Both Worlds?* Windsor: NFER-NELSON.

THOMAS. K. (1984). 'Intercultural relations in the classroom'. In: CRAFT, M. (Ed.) *Education and Cultural Pluralism*. Lewes: Falmer Press.

TOMLINSON, S. (1979). Decision-making in special education (ESN-M) with some reference to children of immigrant parentage. Unpublished PhD thesis, University of Warwick.

TOMLINSON, S. (1982). *A Sociology of Special Education*. London: Routledge and Kegan Paul.

TOMLINSON, S. (1983). *Ethnic Minorities in British Schools*. London: Heinemann.

TOMLINSON, S. (1984). *Home and School in Multicultural Britain*. London: Batsford.

TOMLINSON, S. (1987). 'Towards AD 2000: the political context of multi-cultural education', *New Community*, 14, 1/2, 96–104.

TRACY, M. (1986). 'Initial teacher training and multicultural education', *Journal of Further and Higher Education*, 10, 3, 67–75.

TROYNA, B. (1982). 'The ideological and policy response to black pupils in British schools'. In: HARTNETT, A. (Ed.) *The Social Sciences in Educational Studies*. London: Heinemann.

TROYNA, B. (1984). 'Fact or artefact: the "educational underachievement" of black pupils', *British Journal of Sociology of Education*, 5, 2, 153–66.

TROYNA, B. (1985). 'The "racialization" of contemporary education policy: its origins, nature and impact in a period of contraction', In: WALFORD, G. (Ed.) *Schooling in Turmoil*. Beckenham: Croom Helm.

TROYNA, B (1986). 'Swann's song: the origins, ideology and implications of Education for All', *Journal of Education Policy*, 1, 2, 171–81.

TROYNA, B. (1987). 'Beyond multiculturalism: towards the enactment of antiracist education in policy, provision and pedagogy', *Oxford Review of Education*, 13, 3, 307–20.

TROYNA, B. and BALL, W. (1985). *Views From the Chalk-Face: School Responses to an LEA's Policy on Multicultural Education*, Policy

Papers in Ethnic Relations No. 1, Centre for Research in Ethnic Relations. Coventry: University of Warwick.

TROYNA, B. and CARRINGTON, B. (1987). 'Antisexist/antiracist education – a false dilemma: a reply to Walkling and Brannigan', *Journal of Moral Education*, 16, 1, 60–5.

TROYNA, B. and CARRINGTON, B. (1988). 'Whose side are we on? Ethical dilemmas in research on "race" and education'. In: BURGESS, R. (Ed.) *The Ethics of Educational Research*. Lewes: Falmer Press.

TROYNA, B. and WILLIAMS, J. (1986). *Racism, Education and the State: the Racialization of Education Policy*. Beckenham: Croom Helm.

TUCKER, N. (1981). *The Child and the Book: a Psychological and Literary Exploration*. Cambridge: Cambridge University Press.

UNIVERSITIES COUNCIL FOR THE EDUCATION OF TEACHERS (1986). Teacher education for a multicultural society: UCET Note 1, general principles. London: UCET.

UNIVERSITIES COUNCIL FOR THE EDUCATION OF TEACHERS (1987). CATE. London: UCET

VASSEN, T. (1986). 'Curriculum considerations in the primary school'. In: GUNDARA, J. *et al.* (Eds.) *Racism, Diversity and Education*. London: Hodder and Stoughton.

VYGOTSKY, L.S. (1956). *Selected Psychological Research*. Moscow: Academy of Pedagogic Sciences of USSR.

WALKLING, P.H. and BRANNIGAN, C. (1986) 'Antisexist/antiracist education: a possible dilemma', *Journal of Moral Education*. 15, 1, 6–25.

WARNOCK, M. (1985). 'Teacher teach thyself', *The Listener*, 2 March, 10–12.

WEIGEL, R.H., VERNON, D.T.A. and TOGNACCI, L.N. (1974). 'Specificity of the attitude as a determinant of attitude – behaviour congruence', *Journal of Personality and Social Psychology*, 30, 6, 724–8.

WHITLEY, S. (1988). 'Reading for bias'. In: CARRINGTON, B. and TROYNA, B. (Eds.) *Children and Controversial Issues: Strategies for the Early and Middle Years of Schooling*. Lewes: Falmer Press.

WHITE, P. (1983). *Beyond Domination: An Essay in the Political Philosophy of Education*. London: Routledge and Kegan Paul.

WHYTE, J. (1986). *Girls into Science and Technology*. London: Routledge and Kegan Paul.

WILLEY, R. (1984a). 'Policy responses in education'. In CRAFT, M. (Ed.) *Education and Cultural Pluralism*. Lewes: Falmer Press.

WILLEY, R. (1984b). *Race, Equality and Schools*. London: Methuen.

WILLIAMS, J.E., BEST, D.L., BOSWELL, D.A., MATTSON, L.A. and GRAVES, D.J. (1975). 'Pre-school racial attitude measure 11', *Educational and Psychological Measurement*, 35, 1, 3–18.

WILSON, A. (1981). 'Mixed race children: an exploratory study of racial categorization and identity', *New Community*, 9, 36–43.

WRINGE, C. (1984). *Democracy, Schooling and Political Education*. London: Allen and Unwin.

YEOMANS, A. (1983). 'Collaborative group work in primary and secondary schools', *Durham and Newcastle Research Review*', 10, 95–105.

YOUNG, R.E. (1984). 'Teaching equals indoctrination: the dominant epistemic practices of our schools', *British Journal of Educational Studies*, 22, 3, 220–38.

ZIMET, S.G. (1976). *Print and Prejudice*. London: Hodder and Stoughton.

Name Index

Subject Index